T0318610

Cambridge Elements ≡

Elements in Politics and Society in Southeast Asia
edited by
Edward Aspinall
Australian National University
Meredith L. Weiss
University at Albany, SUNY

DEMOCRATIC DECONSOLIDATION IN SOUTHEAST ASIA

Marcus Mietzner
Australian National University

CAMBRIDGE
UNIVERSITY PRESS

CAMBRIDGE
UNIVERSITY PRESS

University Printing House, Cambridge CB2 8BS, United Kingdom

One Liberty Plaza, 20th Floor, New York, NY 10006, USA

477 Williamstown Road, Port Melbourne, VIC 3207, Australia

314–321, 3rd Floor, Plot 3, Splendor Forum, Jasola District Centre,
New Delhi – 110025, India

79 Anson Road, #06–04/06, Singapore 079906

Cambridge University Press is part of the University of Cambridge.

It furthers the University's mission by disseminating knowledge in the pursuit of education, learning, and research at the highest international levels of excellence.

www.cambridge.org
Information on this title: www.cambridge.org/9781108468954
DOI: 10.1017/9781108677080

© Marcus Mietzner 2021

First published 2021

A catalogue record for this publication is available from the British Library.

ISBN 978-1-108-46895-4 Paperback
ISSN 2515-2998 (online)
ISSN 2515-298X (print)

Democratic Deconsolidation in Southeast Asia

Elements in Politics and Society in Southeast Asia

DOI: 10.1017/9781108677080
First published online: July 2021

Marcus Mietzner
Australian National University, Canberra

Author for correspondence: Marcus Mietzner, mamietzner@yahoo.com

Abstract: Since the mid-2000s, the quality of democracy around the world has been in decline, and Southeast Asia is no exception. This Element analyzes the extent, patterns and drivers of democratic deconsolidation in the three Southeast Asian countries that boast the longest history of electoral democracy in the region: Indonesia, the Philippines and Thailand. While the exact deconsolidation outcomes differ, all three nations have witnessed similar trends of democratic erosion. In each case, long-standing democratic deficiencies (such as clientelism, politicized security forces and non-democratic enclaves) have persisted; rising wealth inequality has triggered political oligarchization and subsequent populist responses embedded in identity politics; and ambitious middle classes have opted for non-democratic alternatives to safeguard their material advancement. As a result, all three polities have descended from their democratic peaks between the late 1980s and early 2000s, with few signs pointing to a return to previous democratization paths.

Keywords: Indonesia; Philippines; Thailand; democracy; authoritarianism

ISBNs: 9781108468954 (PB), 9781108677080 (OC)
ISSNs: 2515-2998 (online), 2515-298X (print)

Contents

1 Introduction

The outbreak of the COVID-19 pandemic has presented significant challenges to democracies around the world, with some leaders using the opportunity to maximize their power and silence oppositional forces (Diamond 2020a). While even established democracies have been affected, younger post-authoritarian states have shown to be particularly vulnerable towards these autocratization attempts. This is because such polities typically do not (yet) possess well-entrenched democratic institutions, and autocratic actors left over from the previous regime remain deeply rooted in society. Southeast Asia has been no exception in this regard. Three of the region's democracies that emerged as a result of the 'third wave' of democratization in the 1980s and 1990s (namely, the Philippines, Thailand and Indonesia) saw their democratic quality declining during the COVID-19 pandemic. In the Philippines, populist President Rodrigo Duterte was given emergency powers that opposition groups described as a 'virtual blank check' (Holmes and Hutchcroft 2020). Similarly, while the Thai government's declaration of a state of emergency helped it to successfully contain the spread of the virus, it also facilitated a 'clampdown on free speech' (HRW 2020). In Indonesia, finally, the national police issued a circular in early April 2020 that asked its officers to particularly scrutinize citizen 'insults' of the president and other state officials over the handling of the pandemic (Ghaliya 2020).

However, while the COVID-19 pandemic has accelerated processes of democratic decline in Southeast Asia's third-wave democracies, it did not trigger them. Indeed, in all three countries, democratic erosion was taking place long before the pandemic began. This suggests that leaders aiming to pursue their illiberal ambitions during the pandemic found it particularly easy to do so in polities already damaged by prior anti-democratic campaigns (Croissant 2020). In this pattern of pre-pandemic democratic decline, Southeast Asia once again reflects a much broader trend. Starting in 2006, there had been an intense debate among democracy scholars about the existence and extent of a global democratic recession. This debate focused on the question of whether democracy, globally and as a system, was receding or whether these depictions were needlessly overdrawn. The first camp in this debate believed that the quality of democracy was indeed eroding. Larry Diamond, leading this group, maintained in 2015 that 'the world has been in a mild but protracted democratic recession since about 2006' (Diamond 2015: 144). The authors of the main democracy indexes tended to agree with Diamond. The Economist's 2019 Democracy Index (The Economist 2019), for instance, recorded 'the worst average global score since the index was first produced in 2006'. Similarly, the

2020 Freedom in the World report warned that '2019 was the 14th consecutive year of decline in global freedom' (Freedom House 2020).

But other authors held a more optimistic view. Wolfgang Merkel (2014: 18), for instance, claimed that analysing the data from several democracy indexes between 1990 and 2010 'does not give any evidence to the crisis hypothesis'. Even in 2018, when the post-2010 data had become available, he asked whether 'the crisis of democracy [is] an invention of theoreticians ... in pursuit of an exaggerated normative democratic ideal?' (Merkel 2018a: 3). Answering this question, he and his co-authors concluded that 'there is no general crisis of democracy but nonsimultaneous developments across different partial regimes and countries that have strengthened and weakened the quality and stability of advanced democracies' (Merkel 2018b). To some extent, Merkel's conclusions are the result of his exclusive focus on 'advanced' democracies (as opposed to Diamond, who included polities with a wide range of democratic quality). But this difference in scope only partly explains the gap between Diamond's and Merkel's judgments, given that the democracy indexes picked up declines in established democracies as well.

Even among those who believed that a pre-pandemic democratic crisis was taking place, there were significant differences when it came to identifying the causes. Some were searching for causes within democracies themselves, such as an increasing crisis of public trust in democratic institutions (Schmidt 2015); escalating inequality (Solt 2008); the struggle of political parties to stay relevant in politics (van Biezen 2014); the rise of identity politics, unleashed partly by social media (Bennett 2012); or apathy with routine democratic procedures, including elections (Blais, Gidengil, Nevitte and Nadeau 2004). Others, by contrast, focused on democracy's enemies that were intent on eroding it, such as populists (Barr 2009); autocratic strongmen (Lancaster 2014); anti-immigration groups (van Spanje 2010); or oligarchs – and other veto players[1] – who use their power to distort democratic processes (Winters 2011). In short, the debate concentrated on the question of whether democracy was destabilizing itself, or whether it was being destabilized.

While the outbreak of COVID-19 has disrupted this scholarly discussion somewhat, understanding the global patterns of pre-pandemic democratic decline remains key to analysing the trajectory of democracy during the crisis response and its aftermath. In fact, in many cases, it was the particular nature of

---

[1] Veto players are defined here as individual or collective actors who have the power to extort significant policy or material concessions from central political institutions, often in exchange for lending legitimacy and support to these institutions. Thus, the definition used here does not rise to Tsebelis' (2002: 19) definitional threshold of a veto player as an actor 'whose agreement is necessary to change the status quo'.

a polity's pre-pandemic democratic erosion that shaped the way its leaders responded to the COVID-19 crisis. Indonesia, with its host of democratic deficiencies, and the United States, where President Donald Trump attempted systematically to dismantle democratic institutions, are two prime examples of polities in which a pre-pandemic democratic crisis predetermined a poor response to the COVID-19 outbreak (Diamond 2020b; Mietzner 2020a). Similarly, the dynamics of democratic decline prior to the pandemic are intrinsically linked to the effectiveness with which leaders tried to use the COVID-19 crisis to their political advantage, and they are certain to influence the character of democratic life in the post-pandemic order as well.

This Element studies Southeast Asia as a case of pre-pandemic democratic decline. It asks whether democracy in the region was indeed in decline prior to the COVID-19 outbreak; if so, what the extent of that decline was; what its drivers were; and, finally, what Southeast Asia tells us about patterns of global democratic recession. Southeast Asia and specific countries within it were chosen as a case study of democratic crisis for two main reasons. First, historically, the region has shown patterns of democratization similar to those in other world regions. It largely followed both the trend of postcolonial democratic enthusiasm and of the authoritarian surge of the 1950s, 1960s and 1970s. Some of its key countries were then also part of the third wave of democratization in the 1980s and 1990s. Thus, analysing democratic quality in Southeast Asia can deliver insights into broader global trends. Second, unlike Eastern Europe or Latin America, which have largely uniform political systems (parliamentarism and presidentialism respectively), Southeast Asia's political regime types differ widely. In the same vein, the level of economic development of the region's countries is highly diverse, as are their religious patterns. Accordingly, choosing Southeast Asia based on both similarities with other world regions and high levels of internal diversity (Ebbinghaus 2005) allows for an analysis of democratic decline patterns beyond country-specific characteristics.

Conceptually, this Element is most interested in how *democracies* declined prior to the pandemic – and not so much in how some electoral authoritarian regimes (such as Cambodia) slipped towards full autocracy or how others (such as Myanmar and Malaysia) started democratic transitions that were eventually aborted. As Diamond pointed out, this latter set of questions is highly relevant too, but at the heart of the global debate on eroding democratic resilience is the discussion of the specific mechanisms through which democracies get damaged. Thus, this Element uses the lens of democratic consolidation and deconsolidation theory to assess trends of pre-pandemic democratic decline in Southeast Asia's post-authoritarian polities. The usage of this analytical frame provides, in comparison to alternative approaches, a stronger focus on the question of how and when decline happens in democratic systems. By contrast, a broader approach of looking at democratic erosion trends – such as the concept of autocratization (Lührmann and Lindberg 2019) – would force us also to explore the decline of democratic quality in autocracies and semi-democracies, which operate under very different conditions. The concept of democratic backsliding, for its part, focuses on 'state-led debilitation' of democracies (Bermeo 2016: 5), missing other, more structural drivers captured by the deconsolidation paradigm. Consequently, this Element discusses only those countries in Southeast Asia that experienced processes of democratic consolidation in their contemporary histories: Indonesia, the Philippines and Thailand.

In its analysis, this Element finds much evidence in Southeast Asia for pre-pandemic democratic deconsolidation. None of the three Southeast Asian countries that began processes of democratic consolidation between the late 1980s and early 2000s was able to sustain its levels of progress, and all have fallen back behind their past democratic peaks. The Element argues that three major factors toxically coincided to produce the outcome of deconsolidation. The first is a set of long-term structural democratic deficiencies that prevented the three polities from turning their early successes of consolidation into further progress. These weaknesses are: persistent clientelistic structures in society and politics; the ongoing politicization of the security forces; and the existence – even at times of democratic peaks – of autocratic enclaves in the broader polity. On their own, however, such defects do not necessarily lead to deconsolidation – they often just result in democratic stagnation or slower progress. In the cases examined here, deconsolidation occurred when these deficiencies combined with the second factor: that is, rising inequality and the politicization of this inequality (mostly by a populist) in the vocabulary of each country's main identity cleavage. Finally, the long-term impact of this democratic crisis has been sustained by the third factor: namely, a middle class endorsing non-democratic alternatives to secure its material and social status.

The rest of this introduction reviews some important works on the decline of democracy in Southeast Asia; introduces the concepts of democratic consolidation and deconsolidation; explains the selection of the specific countries of analysis; and lays out the structure of this Element.

1.1 Crisis of Democracy in Southeast Asia?

Within the broader debate on a pre-pandemic global recession of democracy, there was an extensive discussion prior to the COVID-19 outbreak about whether such democratic erosion was taking place in Southeast Asia as well. These discussions were hardly surprising, given that the region has traditionally been viewed as a difficult place for democratic practices to take root in (Slater

2008; Rodan 2018). The serial collapses of democracies in Southeast Asia in the 1950s, 1960s and 1970s; the long period of almost ubiquitous authoritarianism from the 1970s to the 1990s; the continued endurance of many autocratic regimes since then; and events such as the Thai coups of 2006 and 2014 have made Southeast Asia a highly unlikely candidate for successful, cross-regional democratization. Thus, amid a rich literature on democracy's poor record in Southeast Asia, it is only natural that some academic publications picked up the theme of a (new) democratic crisis in the region in the early 2010s, beginning a discourse that stretched to the COVID-19 outbreak in 2019.

The scholarly contributions to this debate were diverse in their approaches and their identification of possible causes of democratic crises. Chambers and Croissant (2010), for instance, traced the crisis of democracy in Southeast Asia to unresolved problems in the civil–military relations of its key countries. Croissant and Bünte (2011) broadened this perspective, but argued that the crisis of democracy in Southeast Asia was a crisis of democratic governance – thus excluding other possible factors. Conversely, Banpasirichote Wungaeo, Rehbein and Wun'gaeo (2016) offered a wide range of explanatory propositions for democracy's difficulties in Southeast Asia, from 'the legacy of the Cold War, rapid economic development and liberalization, external economic globaliza-tion, the important role of informal politics, powerful elites, and weak but emerging middle classes'. Increasingly, authors have also looked at the compe-tition between China and the United States as a driver of democratic crisis in Southeast Asia (Stromseth and Marston 2019: 7). While differing in their specific emphases, all these works agreed that Southeast Asian democracy was indeed trapped in a new crisis, following episodes of democratization in the 2000s. Slater (2017) presented the most pessimistic of these views, writing that 'it feels in Southeast Asia as if democracy could readily be extinguished entirely'.

Others were less gloomy. Thomas Pepinsky (2020: 1), for example, con-cluded that: '[T]here is no evidence of region-wide democratic erosion in Southeast Asia, in either the short or medium term.' Similarly, some avoided the term 'crisis' altogether, preferring instead to speak of 'challenges' to Southeast Asian democracy. One contribution (Kofi Annan Foundation 2017: 10) found that: '[W]hile an increasing number of ASEAN countries have transitioned towards or adopted democracy . . ., the region still has a difficult relationship with democratic practice.' Although easily dismissible as policy speak, this position took a longer term view, highlighting that ASEAN housed no democracies at all in the late 1960s and 1970s, while there are at least some today. Another more positive angle on the Southeast Asian democracy theme emerged after the elections in Malaysia in May 2018, which (temporarily) removed the country's hegemonic ruling coalition from power after more than sixty years. John Watts (2018) called this event, in combination with another competitive election held in East Timor in the same month, a 'cause to celebrate democracy in Southeast Asia'. Indonesia, he pointed out, also completed another round of local elections at about the same time. Others again, such as Case (2017), have differentiated between the various countries, highlighting democratic collapse in Thailand while praising democracy's durability in Indonesia. Is, therefore, the picture of Southeast Asian democracy being stuck in a serious crisis overdrawn?

Embedding itself within this debate about the state of Southeast Asia's pre-pandemic democracy, this Element offers a conceptual and systematic assessment of when the region's democracies saw peaks in their democratic quality; the extent to which this democratic quality has deteriorated over time; and the factors behind this trend. The analysis will also show how pre-pandemic developments in Southeast Asian democracies aligned with illiberal actions of their leaders during their particular COVID-19 responses. As indicated, the paradigmatic frame for this analysis is the theory of democratic consolidation and deconsolidation. The following subsections explain why Linz and Stepan's notion of consolidation, if revised and extended by newer theories of deconsolidation, can equip the analysis of democratic decline in Southeast Asia with effective tools of assessment and interpretation.

1.2 Democratic Consolidation and its Critics

As stated above, this Element is primarily concerned with assessing how Southeast Asian *democracies* declined prior to the pandemic – as opposed to analysing changes in democratic quality in the region's many autocracies and semi-democracies. For this approach, the paradigm of democratic deconsolidation is best positioned to deliver useful insights, as it focuses strictly on the internal dynamics of declining democracies. It is therefore imperative to start the exploration of democratic consolidation and deconsolidation in pre-pandemic Southeast Asia by introducing clear definitions. Chief among them is the definition of democratic consolidation – the contrasting but inseparably linked counterpart of deconsolidation. Among the definitions of democratic consolidation, the most prominent remains that developed by Juan Linz and Alfred Stepan. Based on their conceptual criteria, a democracy can be considered consolidated if no significant actors try to erect a non-democratic order or secede from the state; if a majority of the public supports democracy and rejects anti-system alternatives; and if resolving conflicts within the constitutional regulations set by the democratic state becomes the norm (Linz and Stepan 1996: 16).

This definition, and the frame within which it was placed, soon attracted criticism. Most of the critiques focused on the democratic consolidation model's supposed assumption of a teleological, linear development of democracy towards a fixed end state, namely consolidation. Guillermo O'Donnell, for instance, argued that the notion of consolidation sets an idealized goal that all democracies were (wrongly) assumed to move towards. 'This mode of reasoning', O'Donnell (1996: 38) maintained, 'carries a strong teleological flavor. Cases that have not "arrived" at full institutionalization, or that do not seem to be moving in this direction, are seen as stunted, frozen, protractedly unconsolidated, and the like.' Thus, he claimed, there were only two categories in the consolidation model: first, a vague category of 'unconsolidated' and, second, an idealized aim of 'consolidation'. While some of the critiques overstated the flaws in Linz and Stepan's model, they helped highlight three issues that it indeed overlooked or underemphasized: first, consolidation was conceptualized as a status rather than a process; second, it did say very little about the stages of consolidation that a democratizing polity has to pass; and, third, it underestimated the possibility of regression or deconsolidation.

Based on these critiques, a number of consolidation scholars amended the Linz and Stepan model in order to save the consolidation paradigm. Larry Diamond (1999: 65), for instance, clarified that consolidation was a process rather than a status. Taking this clarification further, Wolfgang Merkel (1998: 39–40), offered a sequential concept of consolidation featuring four stages: first, the establishment of constitutional organs and political institutions, including the electoral system and the catalogue of civil rights; second, the consolidation of the party system and of interest groups; third, behavioural change among veto actors; and, fourth, anchoring of democratic values among civil society and the broader population. With his model, Merkel established that consolidation is a staged process; that it requires certain preconditions to be fulfilled before consolidation can move to the next level; and that this process is reversible if progress in any of the four stages is rolled back. But while Merkel generally viewed the four stages as sequential, he was not dogmatic about this assumption. It is clear that there are overlaps – and interactions – between the various phases. This dynamism in Merkel's model – while overcoming some of the weaknesses inherent in Linz and Stepan's concept – make it a suitable analytical framework for this study. Most importantly, it will be used to measure democratic consolidation and deconsolidation in the examined case studies.

In spite of such modifications to the consolidation model, the impact of the initial attacks remained significant. In essence, the criticism marginalized the concept of democratic consolidation from the centre of democratic theory. To be sure, a number of writers continued to use various elements of Linz and Stepan's work – such as the discussion on linkages between prior regime type and transition outcome – and students of democracy continued to read and apply their work (Maeda 2016; Kostelka 2017). But the notion of democratic consolidation quickly went out of fashion and was replaced by research on 'democracy with adjectives' (such as illiberal, deliberative, delegative or defective democracy) or on combinations between democracy and autocracy (such as competitive or electoral authoritarianism). However, in the context of rising populism and democratic crises, the notion of democratic consolidation has triggered new interest. This is because some authors have introduced the concept of democratic deconsolidation, which builds on but significantly revises the Linz and Stepan framework. And because there can be no deconsolidation without prior consolidation, Linz and Stepan are – as the next subsection demonstrates – again in the spotlight of comparative democracy studies.

1.3 Democratic Deconsolidation

In 2016 and 2017, Roberto Stefan Foa and Yascha Mounk published two articles in *Journal of Democracy* that introduced the idea that democratic deconsolidation was taking place in many democracies around the world. Foa and Mounk (2017a: 9) proposed that democratic deconsolidation occurs if democracy ceases 'to be the only game in town [and] when, at some later point, a sizable minority of citizens loses its belief in democratic values, becomes attracted to authoritarian alternatives, and starts voting for "antisystem" parties, candidates, or movements that flout or oppose constitutive elements of liberal democracy'. Thus, Foa and Mounk focused on the scenario that Linz and Stepan ignored, at least according to their critics: that is, the possibility that democracies can not only consolidate, but that they are just as able to regress or deconsolidate.

With their approach, Foa and Mounk added previously missing links to the Linz and Stepan model of democratic consolidation. While they did not invent the term 'deconsolidation' (see, for instance, McCoy and Smith 1995), Foa and Mounk developed it into a widely applicable concept. If even full democracies can deconsolidate, then this overcomes all three concerns voiced by Linz and Stepan's critics: first, deconsolidation negates the notion of a teleological impetus of consolidation; second, it implies the existence of consolidation phases; and, third, Foa and Mounk not only concede the possibility of established democracies experiencing regression (which Diamond and Merkel had touched on), they made this process their primary analytical focus. Hence, while opening up new areas of inquiry, the introduction of democratic deconsolidation also allows us to revisit Linz and Stepan's concept in a substantially revised and extended form. This is in spite of the fact that Foa and Mounk do not view their work as a revision and extension of the Linz and Stepan model – but as marking its end (Foa and Mounk 2017b: 18). As suggested earlier, however, consolidation and deconsolidation are inseparably linked.

Although highly innovative, Foa and Mounk's description of deconsolidation as a process in which democracy ceases to be the only game in town remains conceptually vague. Thus, this Element spells out their notion of democratic deconsolidation into a more practical definition that locates deconsolidation within the context of a country's previous record of democratic consolidation. Democratic deconsolidation, then, is defined here as *the process through which existing democracies rewind, lose or otherwise fall behind their achievements in democratic development reached during prior phases of consolidation.* Further operationalizing this definition, and borrowing from Merkel, indicators of 'democratic achievements' being lost can be found in regressions in all four stages of consolidation: institution building; party system consolidation; elite behaviour; and the anchoring of democratic values in society. This definition further clarifies that (a) deconsolidation is not the same as democratic reversal, and deconsolidating democracies often retain their status as an electoral democracy (that is, as a minimalist democracy in which electoral competition takes place but other characteristics of a mature democracy are missing); (b) similar to consolidation, deconsolidation must be conceptualized as a staged process; and (c) deconsolidation, just as consolidation, is reversible.

What makes Foa and Mounk's deconsolidation research particularly relevant for this study is their use of post-authoritarian case studies as examples of what could happen to the West's consolidated democracies if they failed to address early warning signs of democratic decline. Foa and Mounk (2017: 10) assert that: '[W]hile the ascent of populist parties and movements is relatively new in North America and Western Europe, other regions show how democratic deconsolidation can signal a real danger for the stability of democratic governance, even in countries that appear to be doing very well according to more traditional measures.' They offer Venezuela and Poland as illustrations, but Southeast Asia's democracies (and former democracies) are suitable case studies as well. This Element analyses selected Southeast Asian polities in the same spirit with which Foa and Mounk looked at Venezuela and Poland. As polities that passed various stages of democratic consolidation in recent times, they deserve to be examined in their own right, but their experiences tell us much about global patterns of democratic development as well.

Foa and Mounk's ideas were met with a wave of protest that was similar in intensity to that attracted by Linz and Stepan twenty years earlier. But most of the critiques were not of a conceptual, but rather of an empirical nature. The thrust of the criticism was that Foa and Mounk exaggerated the extent of democratic decline in Western democracies (Alexander and Welzel 2017;

Norris 2017). However, whether or not Foa and Mounk overstated the risk of democratic decline in long-established democracies is irrelevant for this study. This Element is more interested in Foa and Mounk's choice of polities such as Poland and Venezuela to illustrate the danger of democratic deconsolidation in non-Western democracies, and its potential replication in Western, fully consolidated democracies. This study, then, explores what the Southeast Asian case studies (which in many ways are comparable to Poland and Venezuela) bring to this discussion, regardless of the current state of Western democracies.

1.4 The Case Studies and Structure of this Element

As indicated earlier, this Element focuses on those Southeast Asian countries that have experienced phases of democratic consolidation in their recent political history. In order to identify such countries, the Element uses a simple but effective measure: it includes all countries for which the Freedom in the World index developed by Freedom House recorded the status of 'free' in five consecutive years at any point in their histories after 1973 (when the index began its assessments).[2] While the index assesses freedom rather than democracy, a rating of 'free' in five successive years is a strong indication that some form of consolidation in key areas of democratic development was taking place during that timeframe. Based on this approach, the countries qualifying for evaluation in this Element are Indonesia, which entered a period of democratic consolidation in the 2000s (it was rated 'free' by Freedom House from 2006 to 2013); Thailand, whose democracy peaked in the mid-1990s to early 2000s (it was rated 'free' without interruptions from 1998 to 2004); and the Philippines, which began an early phase of consolidation in the late 1980s (when it was rated 'free' from 1987 to 1989 and then again from 1996 to 2004).

The application of the deconsolidation model, and the criteria mentioned above, obviously lead to the exclusion of Southeast Asian nations that never entered periods of consolidation. This exclusion, while reducing the Element's empirical breadth, is necessary to maintain its analytical depth. For instance, while Myanmar and Malaysia began fragile democratic transitions in 2015 and 2018 respectively, these were ended by Myanmar's military coup in February 2021 and the return to power of Malaysia's former government party in 2020 (which later culminated in the suspension of parliament). Similarly, East Timor is excluded as it received its first 'free' ranking in 2018 and thus has not yet recorded five consecutive 'free' ratings. While some observers saw Cambodia on the path towards democratic

---

[2] Each year, the index classifies countries as 'free', 'partly free' or 'not free', based on an assessment of their political rights and civil liberties.

transition (and possibly consolidation) after 1992 (Curtis 1998), the country quickly descended into restored strongman rule, with only occasional concessions to greater political participation. Finally, full authoritarianism has endured for decades in Vietnam, Laos and Brunei, while Singapore alternates between periods of full and competitive authoritarianism (Weiss 2020). Detecting fluctuations in these countries' approach to democratic opening is an interesting exercise, but is outside the aims of the democratic deconsolidation approach and thus of this Element.

This does not mean, however, that trends in these countries won't be considered when trying to identify broader trends in Southeast Asia's political pre-pandemic trajectory as well as the actors driving it. The reasons that obstructed Myanmar's and Malaysia's democratic transitions or prevented other countries in the region from democratizing at all have been strikingly similar to the reasons why its existing democracies deconsolidated. Whenever such comparisons are useful to the overall analysis, they will be made.

The remainder of this Element is structured as follows. In Section 2, I identity each country's peak of democratic consolidation. This identification of democratic zeniths, which uses Merkel's four criteria of democratic consolidation (as well as V-Dem's Deliberative Democracy scores), is essential to establish a democratic baseline against which later declines can be measured. Section 3 carries out that measurement, comparing each country's democratic peak with its current democratic status. This contrasting assessment of each polity's democratic pinnacle and its current level of democratic quality reveals an overall trend of deconsolidation. Section 4 turns to the analysis of potential causes for this trend, highlighting long-standing structural defects in each country's polity. Section 5 begins with the exposition of newer deconsolidation drivers. Concretely, it posits rising wealth inequality as the socio-economic context of deconsolidation, and explains how this inequality was subsequently politicized by populists within the framework of each country's dominant identity cleavage. Section 6 highlights the role of middle-class voters in sustaining democratic erosion in the three countries, with anxiety over their material status driving affluent citizens to endorse non-democratic actors. The conclusion, in Section 7, summarizes the Element's findings and situates Southeast Asia within the comparative debate of global democratic recession patterns.

2 Democratic Peaks

In order to evaluate the extent of pre-pandemic democratic deconsolidation in Southeast Asian countries, we must first identify the peak of consolidation from which they subsequently descended. It is important to note from the beginning that no Southeast Asian democracy has ever been fully consolidated – at least not by this study's substantive understanding of completed consolidation as laid out in Linz and Stepan's three dimensions. Rather, Southeast Asia's democracies have been in various phases of a consolidation *process*. Deconsolidation, then, is the regression from already achieved levels in this consolidation process – the highest point of this achievement being referred to here as the democratic peak.

Following from this Element's definition of democratic deconsolidation outlined above, Wolfgang Merkel's four-stage model of democratic consolidation is used here as an analytical tool to measure the quality of a country's democratic consolidation and to identify the highest phase of consolidation it reached. Importantly, his model not only delivers criteria against which key conditions of consolidation can be assessed, but it also ties them to particular phases in the process. Recall that these four main criteria and phases are: first, the creation of constitutional and political institutions, such as the electoral system and mechanisms through which civil rights can be protected; second, the consolidation of the party system and of interest groups; third, behavioural change of former and potentially new veto actors, reducing the risk of democratic reversal; and, fourth, anchoring democratic values among civil society and the broader population, firming the ideational basis of the state. Recall also, however, that the sequencing in Merkel's model is not always linear – countries can advance non-sequentially in different stages at varying times, which, in itself, gives clues about the sustainability of the consolidation process. In combination, this set of sequenced conditions forms the conceptual blueprint against which the democratic realities of our three Southeast Asian case studies are evaluated.

The following examination of democratic peaks uses a country-based approach rather than a cross-country evaluation of consolidation phases. This is because the task of this section is to identify consolidation peaks in specific countries. In order to achieve that, Merkel's four criteria need to be applied within the individual democratic narrative of each polity, with the four measurements informing one another. Thus, the section analyses, consecutively, the democratic zeniths of Indonesia, the Philippines and Thailand and concludes with a brief summary of what sustained and ultimately disrupted each of them.

2.1 Indonesia: 2004–8

Indonesia has had two democratic peaks in its history: the first at around 1955 and a second, higher apex between 2004 and 2008. In 1955, Indonesia was in a grey zone between democratic transition and early stages of consolidation: in that year, its appointed parliament was replaced by a freely elected one; citizens participated widely in elections; post-war local conflicts had subsided; political power was shared or rotated between key parties; and the influence of the army, the main potential veto player, was small. But this peak was followed by rapid decline and a full democratic reversal in 1959 (Feith 1962). Most responsible for this were irreconcilable ideological differences between the leading parties; authoritarian ambitions by both President Sukarno and the army; and an explosion of local conflicts after 1956, followed by the imposition of martial law in affected areas.

After four decades of authoritarianism under Sukarno (1959–66) and his successor Suharto (1966–98), Indonesia's second, more contemporary democratic transition began with Suharto's fall. This transition was marked by constitutional reforms, national power struggles, communal conflicts with thousands of fatalities and the secession of East Timor (Aspinall 2005; Mietzner 2009; Horowitz 2013). Nevertheless, the transition was successfully completed in 2004, the year of Indonesia's first direct presidential election. Subsequently, Indonesia entered an early phase of democratic consolidation. But the post-2004 polity quickly peaked with its consolidation drive, recording first signs of stagnation and mild decline by about 2009. Below, we analyse these trends by using Merkel's analytical instruments, identifying the peaks of consolidation in each segmental arena as well as events that ended these democratic highpoints.

To begin with, Indonesia's constitutional organs and political institutions stabilized considerably in 2004 after undergoing much change in the democratic transition period. The constitutional amendments that came into full force in 2004 clarified the role of the presidency and parliament, removing institutional uncertainties highlighted by the chaotic impeachment of President Abdurrahman Wahid in 2001. Basic civil rights protections were also put in place, with a catalogue of universal human rights integrated into the constitution. As indicated above, the post-authoritarian electoral regime took shape in 2004 too. In that year's national elections, the appointment of military members to parliament ceased and the election of the president shifted from an indirect mechanism to a popular vote. In 2005, this was followed by the introduction of direct elections for local government heads, replacing the old system of indirect election by parliament. This change made 2005 the year in which Indonesia's new democratic polity became fully operational and, concurrently, reached the climax of its reform spirit.

But while the constitutional organs, formal civil rights protections and electoral system created during this democratic peak are still in place today, there have been important indications of decline in their quality. Attacks on religious minorities increased after 2005 (Bush 2015), questioning the state's consistency in enforcing civil rights. The electoral system, for its part, began to show signs of qualitative deterioration in the late 2000s, despite continued formal competitiveness. From 2009 onwards, the parliamentary elections switched to a fully open party list system, leading to a spike in vote-buying practices (Aspinall and Sukmajati 2016; Muhtadi 2019). Moreover, state subsidies to political parties participating in elections were reduced in the second half of the 2000s (Mietzner 2015), making such parties more reliant on outside funding. Entry requirements for new electoral parties were gradually tightened, eliminating many of the small parties that had represented minority constituencies in the 1999 and 2004 elections. Overall, after reaching their highest levels of competitiveness in the mid-2000s, Indonesian elections became more personalized, exceedingly expensive and less inclusive.

In Merkel's second arena of democratic consolidation (that of the party system and interest groups), Indonesia's polity of the mid-2000s also initially showed signs of institutional deepening. Unlike many other polities emerging from decades of authoritarianism, Indonesia had some well-developed party structures in place when Suharto fell, and it had functioning socio-religious organizations that could establish new parties and thus properly represent the country's cleavage system (King 2003). Furthermore, the 1999 and 2004 parliamentary elections were held under a proportional representation system with a closed and a semi-open party list respectively – that is, a system that strengthened parties over individual candidates. Relatively lax registration and parliamentary thresholds also allowed smaller parties to operate, securing a substantial degree of representativeness in the party system. High party identification levels (i.e. a large percentage of voters who felt close to any of the existing parties) signalled strong acceptance of the party system. In 2004, party identification stood at 54 per cent; while this was lower than in 1999, it was still a lot higher than that in many Western democracies at that time. Concurrently, interest groups also mushroomed – labour unions and professional associations enjoyed their new freedoms after long periods of tight regulation and control during previous authoritarian regimes. Indeed, their problem soon became excessive fragmentation rather than repression (Caraway and Ford 2020).

But the changes in the electoral system that weakened the latter from the late 2000s onwards also began to undermine the effectiveness of the party system. The introduction of the fully open party list system strengthened individual candidates over parties; the reduction in party subsidies helped opening the door to oligarchs interested in establishing or taking over parties; and ever-increasing thresholds to new party creations ruled out financially less powerful actors from participating in party politics. Socially rooted parties, which had dominated the 1999 and 2004 elections, gradually had to accept the rise of personalist and oligarchic parties, which were created only to facilitate the political ambitions of their leaders (Tomsa 2010). The shrinking of political opportunity space led to a consolidation of the party system as far as the declining numbers of parties was concerned, but that came at the cost of decreasing political representativeness. As a result, the party identification levels began to decline (they reached 18 per cent by 2009), demonstrating that party system strength had passed its zenith (Mietzner 2013: 44). Interest groups did not face the same decline in solidity and relevance, but they too found it difficult to translate their societal power into political influence.

In the mid-2000s, there was also clearly behavioural change within former and potential veto powers – the indicator Merkel views as the third phase of consolidation. To be sure, much of this change was imposed on veto powers by assertive civilian actors. The country's most influential veto power, the military, was politically marginalized for much of the mid-2000s, although it held on to some residual privileges (such as de facto impunity from persecution for its past and present human rights violations). The removal of the military from parliament in 2004 was accompanied by the Aceh peace accord in 2005, which was negotiated against strong opposition from within the officer corps (Aspinall 2009). But afterwards, President Susilo Bambang Yudhoyono, who ruled from 2004 to 2014, relaxed his control over the military again. For instance, he offered the armed forces a compromise on the regulation of military businesses in 2009. In the same vein, Islamist political actors – who, as a group, constituted another potential veto power – were sidelined during the presidency of Megawati Sukarnoputri (2001–4) and in the very early Yudhoyono period. Subsequently, however, Yudhoyono allowed conservative Islamic organizations, such as the Indonesian Council of Islamic Scholars (MUI), to grow into powerful veto forces during the rest of his rule (Mietzner and Muhtadi 2018).

The most difficult consolidation criterion to verify is Merkel's fourth indicator and stage: namely, the extent to which democratic values have been anchored in civil society and the broader population. While hard to grasp as a single category, we can nevertheless find a significant degree of post-authoritarian enthusiasm for democracy in the late 1990s to the mid-2000s, as reflected in high approval ratings for democracy; strong party identification numbers; consistently solid voter turnout; and – by about 2004 – the end of the ethno-religious mass conflict that had plagued the transition. But, as is the case in most young democracies, the rootedness of democratic values was volatile and thus vulnerable to fluctuation and erosion. By the late 2000s, it became clear that Islamic conservatism in society was growing (or at least more aggressively displayed), leading to slow but important value changes that undermined the anchoring of democratic norms. For instance, a survey in the early 2010s showed that 72 per cent of Indonesian Muslims wanted Islamic law to become the 'law of the land', and 50 per cent stated that it should be applied to non-Muslims as well (Pew Research Center 2013: 46, 48).

The application of the Merkel criteria, then, confirms that Indonesian democracy had entered an early phase of consolidation in 2004 and progressed further moderately until about 2008. The beginning of this phase was marked by the presidential elections of 2004, and its end by rising attacks on religious minorities and the electoral changes of 2009. In terms of the sequencing of consolidation, Indonesia made most progress during that period in the field of establishing constitutional organs and effective electoral and party systems; had moderate success in side-lining veto powers; and struggled to anchor democratic values substantively in society. Importantly, key democracy indexers echo this assessment of democratic consolidation in Indonesia peaking between 2004 and 2008. Freedom House's Freedom in the World index, for instance, saw strong increases for Indonesia between 2003 and 2006, but it subsequently peaked at a total aggregate score of sixty-seven points in 2008 – a level it has not achieved since. Similarly, V-Dem's Deliberative Democracy index (which captures the democratic quality of decision-making beyond the formality of electoral procedures)[3] recorded an all-time high of 0.67 in 2004, gradually falling to 0.55 in the mid- and late 2010s (see Figure 1).[4]

2.2 Philippines: 1987–90

Similarly to Indonesia, the Philippines experienced an early postcolonial democratic peak in the 1950s and 1960s and a more contemporary one much later – in its case, in the late 1980s. From 1947 to the late 1960s, the country was in a democratic transition phase bordering on early consolidation, arguably peaking under the presidency of Ramon Magsaysay (1953–7). Magsaysay ended the long, largely peasant-driven Huk rebellion, and while he 'died in a plane crash in 1957, [he] remained the Filipino's model of a caring, pro-masses president' (Romeo and Guerrero 2008: 2). Indeed, many at the time viewed the Philippines as the 'ultimate third world democracy' (Overholt 2017), holding regular and competitive elections, albeit with low registration rates. But while democratic

---

[3] More concretely, V-Dem (2015: 5) posits the deliberative component of democracy as 'the core value that political decisions in pursuit of the public good should be informed by respectful and reasonable dialogue at all levels rather than by emotional appeals, solidary attachments, parochial interests, or coercion'.

[4] For comparison, Germany – as a liberal democracy – recorded a value of 0.79 in 2019.

Figure 1 V-Dem Deliberative Democracy Index for Indonesia, 1900–2019

quality remained moderately high until the re-election of Ferdinand Marcos in 1969, the weaknesses of the country's institutions – hurriedly copied from its former colonial power, the United States – became abundantly clear in Marcos' second term. Marcos declared martial law in 1972 and ruled as an autocrat until his toppling by an uprising in 1986.

The Philippines began its modern-day post-authoritarian transition with the presidential inauguration of Corazon Aquino in 1986. The democratic transition was successfully 'completed after the May 1987 congressional and January 1988 local elections' (Thompson 1996: 180), leading into an early consolidation phase. This immediate post-Marcos consolidation period, starting in 1987 and ending in about 1990 – when 'high hopes [gave] way to cynicism and even despair' (Freedom House 1991: 14) – marks the Philippines' contemporary democratic peak. During that time, the implementation of a new constitution in 1987 allowed for the rebuilding of the democratic organs destroyed under Marcos. Among others, the 1987 constitution limited the presidency to one term and restored a competitive electoral regime. The new elections framework left many problems untouched (such as the dominance of land-owning clans), but it established a functional basis for electoral democracy. Thus, despite the gradual dissipation of pro-democracy enthusiasm after 1990, electoral democracy remained in place under the presidencies of Fidel Ramos (1992–8) and Joseph Estrada (1998–2001). The temporary collapse of democracy came only in 2004, when then President Gloria Arroyo Macapagal was widely believed to have conspired with the military and the Electoral Commission to inflate her vote result and illegitimately secure re-election (Hutchcroft 2008).

In the early post-Marcos democratic peak, civil rights were enshrined in the 1987 constitution, drawing from the lessons of the authoritarian period. Determined to put these new protections into practice, Corazon Aquino engaged in intense efforts to end the human rights violations against many long-term dissidents of the state. She approved the January 1987 Jeddah peace accord with Muslim rebels in Mindanao, and pursued an arrangement with the Communist Party of the Philippines (CCP) and its armed wing, the New People's Army (NPA). Aquino released key CCP leaders from prison soon after coming to power, hoping to end their rebellion, which had begun in the early 1970s. But the CCP-NPA insurgency quickly intensified again, as did the rebellion in Mindanao, triggering renewed violations of civil rights. Thus, while broadly upheld in the first few years after the fall of Marcos, state protections for civil rights were not institutionalized – especially in conflict areas, where they are most needed. All post-Aquino presidents made renewed attempts at resolving the Mindanao, CCP and other political conflicts, with the results ranging from outright failure to volatile peace settlements.

The Philippines has a traditionally fragmented party system with high levels of party hopping (Kimura 1991; Hicken 2014), and this did not change during the transition and early consolidation. Although Corazon Aquino had come to power supported by the multiparty alliance United Nationalist Democratic Organization (UNIDO), and there was hence a solid pro-democracy grouping in the early post-authoritarian party system, this coalition splintered into its various elements as early as 1987. Concurrently, the older parties suppressed under Marcos' martial law regime (the UNIDO-affiliated Liberal and Nacionalista Parties) did not recover quickly from authoritarianism, while Marcos' political vehicle Kilusang Bagong Lipunan (KBL) shrank to mini-party status (this stood in sharp contrast to Indonesia, where Suharto's regime party Golkar remained a key actor). Therefore, the party system emerging from the Marcos era was unstable, with new parties rapidly emerging and vanishing. Nevertheless, while the post-1986 party system returned to its traditional weakness, it was strong enough to provide an arena for democratic competition after the Marcos era. In the same vein, interest groups mushroomed after Marcos' fall, and although they struggled against the influence of the old social forces of the Philippines (such as the land-owning clans), they soon took their place as important actors of Philippine democracy (Hedman 2006: 2).

There was also significant change in veto power behaviour in the 1987–90 period. As in the Indonesian case, this change was mostly enforced on them rather than naturally accepted. As in Indonesia, too, the armed forces were the biggest potential spoiler of democratic reform. In 1986 and 1987, Aquino faced no fewer than six mutinies and coup attempts, with the most serious one failing in August 1987 (Hernandez 1988). But for the following two and a half years, until December 1989, there were no military mutinies, signifying a period of stability. The temporary ceasefires with the CCP-NPA and the Mindanao rebels also meant that the military briefly lost some of its strategic importance. This changed, however, with the re-intensification of the armed conflicts in the late 1980s and early 1990s, which increased the government's dependence on the military. The election of former military leader Fidel Ramos to the presidency in 1992 reflected the armed forces' grown influence, as well as a festering frustration in the electorate with civilian politics. The other influential veto power, consisting of the deeply entrenched clans and local bosses (Sidel 1999), was left mostly untouched in the Aquino-Ramos period, as Aquino herself belonged to a big clan and Ramos also came from a political family. In return, the clans refrained (temporarily at least) from openly sabotaging the institutional democratization presided over by members of their own class.

The extent to which democratic values were rooted in society during this period is, as in the Indonesian case, subject to debate. Nominally, support for democracy in opinion surveys was high, voter turnout strong and political activism extraordinarily intense for the standards of the Southeast Asian region. But one particular item included in opinion surveys from the 1980s seems to most accurately capture the democratic mood of the period. A regular survey done by the Bishops-Businessmen's Conference for Human Development (BBC) asked whether people felt they could freely express their opinion and criticize the government (Mangahas 2019). The highest level ever reached in that category was in March 1987, just after the new constitution was ratified (the number of respondents who felt that their freedom of expression was secured was sixty-three points higher than those who didn't). One and a half years later, however, this 'net freedom' had declined to sixteen points, showing how fast the Philippines' democratic peak was passing. While these numbers subsequently fluctuated, they never reached the 1987 levels again. In line with this trend, later opinion surveys (conducted in the early 2000s) picked up a growing prioritization of economic development over democracy. In 2003, for example, only 12 per cent agreed that 'democracy is definitely more important', while 68 per cent stated that "economic development is definitely more important" (Abueva and Guerro 2003: 12).

The above analysis supports the classification of the early post-Marcos period as the Philippines' recent democratic peak. The democratic constitution was finalized quickly; the party system was weak but sustained the functioning of electoral democracy; veto players were kept temporarily in check; and opinion polls suggested that the public felt liberal freedoms were upheld. But, by the early 1990s, armed conflicts had resumed, the military's influence increased, and public satisfaction with democracy declined. This does not mean that democratic quality collapsed dramatically after 1990. Indeed, some indexes view the Ramos, Estrada and Benigno Aquino (2010–16) presidencies as rivalling the early post-Marcos period in democratic substance. But our discussion showed that much of the momentum of pro-democracy reform had been lost by the early 1990s, and a close reading of the Freedom House index confirms this narrative. In the index, the Philippines achieved its peak rating of two in both civil liberties and political rights in 1987, but subsequently declined and lost its status of 'free' in 1990. Even after reaching 'free' status again in the late 1990s and early 2000s, the Philippines never achieved a rating of two in both civil liberties and political rights again. The V-Dem's Deliberative Democracy index sees more fluctuation over time, but it too agrees that the later Arroyo and Duterte presidencies saw the Philippines falling behind its 1987–90 democratic achievements, emphasizing a clear deconsolidation curve. Concretely, the Philippines score in this index fell from 0.52 in 1990 to 0.41 in 2019 (see Figure 2).

2.3 Thailand: 1998–2002

In its political history, Thailand has had one clearly identifiable democratic peak: that is, a phase of democratic consolidation between 1998 and 2002. Its other democratic periods were phases of democratic transition, either completed (1992–7) or failed (1973–6, 2011–14). In between these brief episodes of democratic consolidation and completed or failed transitions, there have been extended periods of military rule and/or tutelage. This includes the current phase of indirect military tutelage, with the electoral and broader political system still heavily manipulated in favor of the former military junta that was in power between 2014 and 2019. Therefore, in line with this section's focus on identifying and assessing democratic highpoints in a country's political trajectory, the discussion below concentrates on the consolidation phase of the late 1990s and early 2000s. This phase, in turn, followed the democratic transition which began with the 1992 fall of the military regime of Suchinda Kraprayoon and was completed with the passing of the 1997 constitution. During the early phase of post-1997 democratic consolidation, Thailand saw increased political competition ahead of the 2001 elections; the holding of those elections; and the coming to power of the populist Thaksin Shinawatra, who gained office with a democratic landslide in 2001. This 1998–2002 peak of consolidation ended with Thaksin's increasing authoritarian ambitions shortly after winning the 2001 ballot.

Philippines

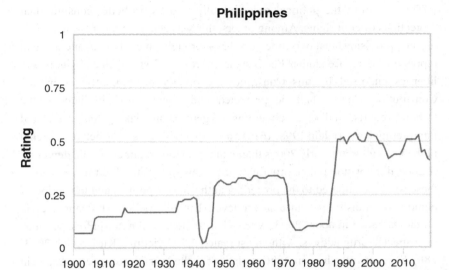

Figure 2 V-Dem Deliberative Democracy Index for the Philippines, 1900–2019

The beginning of Thailand's democratic consolidation process was marked by the finalization of the 1997 constitution, which was widely acknowledged as the most democratic in the country's history (Klein 1998; Harding 2001). The constitution re-arranged Thailand's political institutions, reducing the power of the military and dramatically increasing that of democratically elected politicians. In that spirit, it revamped Thailand's electoral system. Aimed to reduce vote buying, party hopping and unstable governments, the 1997 reforms 'changed [the electoral mechanism] from a multiple-seat constituency system to a combination of … single-seat electoral constituencies and … party-list proportional [representation]' (Yoshifumi 2014: 102). This system gave Thaksin, the clear election winner in 2001, a strong plurality to form a stable government. Prior to and after the 2005 elections, however, the system's weaknesses became apparent, as Thaksin tried to misuse his electoral dominance to monopolize power (Kuhonta 2008). He launched libel suits against opposition lawmakers, pushed through business deals that favoured his companies and withdrew government advertisements from critical press outlets. Ultimately, Thaksin's 'arrogant and authoritarian streak' (Hewison 2010: 123) undermined the competitiveness – and therefore credibility and sustainability – of the very electoral system that had facilitated his rise.

The reform of the political order initially also led to better constitutional protections of civil rights. Among others, this was achieved by creating constitutional provisions that overrode prior laws through which the bureaucracy had repressed liberal freedoms. For instance, Article 27 stated that: 'Rights and liberties endorsed by this Constitution explicitly or implicitly, or by the Constitution Court, shall be protected and legally bind Parliament, the Cabinet, courts, and other government agencies in making, enforcing and interpreting laws' (Klein 1998: 16). As a result, civil rights were better protected in the late 1990s and early 2000s than under previous regimes. While democratization did not stop police brutality against suspects and other transgressions, these were – compared to the preceding authoritarian polities and the period of democratic transition – on a lower level. But this period of stronger civic freedoms ended in about 2003, when Thaksin approved extra-judicial killings of suspected drug addicts, with an estimated 2,500 victims (Kurlantzick 2003: 288). Subsequently, human rights violations in the Muslim south re-escalated in 2004, further accelerating the decline of civil rights protections in the later Thaksin era.

Similarly to the Philippines, Thailand began its democratic consolidation period with a notoriously weak party system (Croissant and Völkel 2012). With the exception of the Democrat Party, most Thai parties had been vehicles for military officers to exert political influence and thus were short-lived. But the entry of Thaksin's Thai Rak Thai Party into the system in 1998 seemed to provide new stability to the party landscape. Unlike any party before it, Thai Rak Thai succeeded in bundling the aspirations of many poorer voters, especially in the country's north and northeast, as well as of other 'urbanized villagers' (Thabchumpon and McCargo 2011: 1018). The party's 2001 result (40.6 per cent) was the best performance of any political party since the 1950s. However, Thai Rak Thai's strength eventually turned from an asset into a liability for the party system: prior to the 2005 elections, Thaksin increasingly viewed his party not only as an electoral competitor, but as Thailand's new state party. With smaller parties sidelined, the imbalances within the party system undermined the system's viability. Comparable tendencies occurred in the arena of interest groups as well. Whereas Thaksin initially allowed much space for programmatic proposals advanced by labour unions, for example, he subsequently abandoned this approach in favour of pro-business market policies (Brown and Hewison 2005). Accordingly, the room for interest groups opposed to the government began to shrink.

One of the most prominent features of Thailand's democratic peak in the late 1990s and early 2000s was the restraint shown by Thailand's most influential veto powers: namely, the monarchy and the armed forces. Both had initially stood by as Thaksin established his power in the early 2000s, allowing him to govern without much interference. This was not because they supported Thaksin or competitive democracy in principle – they simply were 'in a position of profound weakness' (McCargo 2005: 516). Thus, in this period, Thailand's veto powers were in their most marginalized state since the 1930s. But the conflicts surrounding the disputed 2005 and 2006 elections – which were challenged by Thaksin's opponents as illegitimate because of his growing anti-democratic behaviour – delivered both actors a pretext on which to fully reengage in the political arena. The reinvigoration of the monarchy-military alliance, or 'network monarchy' (McCargo 2005), led, first, to extra-parliamentary mobilization against Thaksin and, finally, his overthrow by the military in 2006.

In the early 2000s, there also seems to have been a moderate anchoring of democratic values in society, at least for a number of years. In a 2001 survey, many respondents who expressed views of democracy (80 per cent of those who were asked in the survey offered an opinion) showed an understanding of democracy that did not 'differ much from those of European and American respondents' (Albritton and Bureekul 2008: 119). More than half of the responsive survey participants interpreted democracy in terms of civil and political rights, while an additional 26 per cent viewed democracy in an otherwise positive light. There was also clear societal condemnation of the previous regime as dictatorial (78 per cent of respondents thought it was), and an equally evident appreciation for the order existing in 2001 as being democratic – 88 per cent of respondents supported this view (Albritton and Bureekul 2008: 120). But, as in the Indonesian and Philippine cases, the rootedness of these democratic values in society proved volatile – in 2003, many Thais proclaiming to endorse democratic norms saw no problem with concurrently supporting Thaksin's extrajudicial killings of suspected drug pushers.

Thailand's phase of democratic consolidation, then, was based on a strong basis of constitutional reform; a much less stable but nevertheless democratic party system; a meaningful marginalization of the veto players (at least for Thai standards); and a modest degree of democratic value anchoring. As in the case of Indonesia and the Philippines, therefore, the consolidation process was strongest in its first phase and weaker in the subsequent stages and conditions. But however strong this consolidation was between 1998 (the year after the constitution was passed) and 2002 (the year before Thaksin's extra-judicial killings), it is clear that the quality of Thai democracy declined quickly from this peak. According to Freedom House, Thailand's democratic peak lasted until 2004, when the country lost its status as 'free'. In V-Dems' Deliberative Democracy index, 2001 is identified as democracy's peak, but democratic quality is seen as remaining at a high level until 2005 (see Figure 3). But this Element argues that the 2003 extra-judicial killings were such a momentous break from democratic practices that it must be classified as the end of the peak of democratic consolidation in Thailand. Democracy was still in place for three years after the killings, but its prime had passed.

2.4 Sustaining Transitions and Consolidation

The above discussion has shown similar historical patterns of democratic consolidation peaks in the three Southeast Asian countries that have experienced such consolidation. To begin with, in all three countries, their democratic highpoints lie in the recent *past* – that is, none of them is currently recording a peak in its democratic trajectory. What is more, in all three cases, these peaks occurred more than a decade ago. This would suggest that a structural, longer term process of democratic deconsolidation has been and is still occurring – an indication that Section 3 of this Element will aim to substantiate. Furthermore, the application of Merkel's consolidation criteria has pointed to a comparable sequencing of consolidation in the three polities: all three made meaningful progress in constitutional, electoral and institutional reform, accompanied by at least nominal creation of civil rights protections; all three experienced significant difficulties in establishing stable party systems, but saw interest groups mushrooming during democratization; all three succeeded – despite their weak

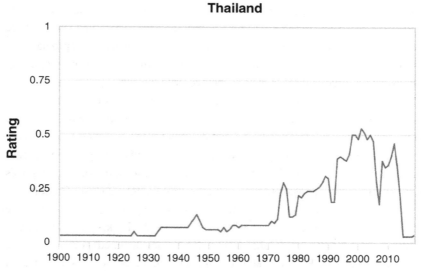

Figure 3 V-Dem Deliberative Democracy Index for Thailand, 1900–2019

party systems – in temporarily sidelining their veto powers; and all three witnessed some extent of proliferation in democratic values, although subsequent developments proved them to be vulnerable to erosion.

In discussing the drivers of the processes outlined above, we need to distinguish three different subject areas: first, factors that helped polities to complete democratic transitions and enter early phases of democratic consolidation; second, conditions that helped democracies to reach the peak of their quality at different points of their consolidation processes; and, third, reasons for the end of and subsequent descent from these democratic peaks.

Successful democratic transitions in Southeast Asia have typically been enabled by a number of features. The first is cross-constituency agreement between key civilian forces on a post-authoritarian constitution (Horowitz 2013). It is crucial to note that other Southeast Asian nations that started democratic transitions but did not complete them (that is, Myanmar and Malaysia) failed precisely in this key effort. The second factor in successful transitions is the holding of at least one democratic election after the first election immediately following or initiating the regime change. These post-transition elections often reflect comprehensive electoral reform projects (leading to reformed elections in 2004 in Indonesia, 1987 in the Philippines and 2001 in Thailand), whereas Malaysia and Myanmar retained the electoral frameworks developed under authoritarianism. The third factor is the effective management or ending of major communal violence (Ganguli 2012). And, fourth, countries with successful transitions see the temporary or long-term marginalization or appeasement of potential veto powers. (Alagappa 2001). Importantly too, all these conditions are more likely to be fulfilled if a country avoids severe economic downturns, and if public satisfaction with government service delivery remains high. Indonesia, the Philippines and Thailand met these criteria as well.

Once consolidation has begun, its further upgrading is dependent on a number of conditions. First, the key stipulations of the post-authoritarian constitution must not only be decided on, but also be put into practice, as they were – for instance – in Indonesia between 2003 and 2005. Second, elites and the public must maintain, in spite of increasing temporal distance to the regime change, their rejection of non-democratic alternatives. And third, monopolization of power in the hands of one actor or institution must be avoided through a regularized and increasingly consolidated division of power, with non-state, social forces assuming crucial scrutinizing roles. In other words, state power must be dispersed and civil society has to be vibrant in order to counterbalance the former (Linz and Stepan 1996; Diamond and Morlino 2004). As in the case of successful transitions, the probability of reaching and sustaining these achievements increases if major economic crises do not occur, and if public service delivery continues to be stable. From the above discussion of democratic peaks and their subsequent end, it is evident that Indonesia, the Philippines and Thailand initially managed to meet all or some of these conditions for a period of time, but at some point began to fail sustaining this success.

While the drivers of democratic deconsolidation are explored in detail in later sections of this Element, it is useful to pinpoint briefly the phenomena that accompanied the descent from democratic peaks in pre-pandemic Southeast Asia. These were a) the return of old veto powers, such as the military and the monarchy in Thailand; b) the decline of competitiveness or credibility of the electoral regime, particularly in Thailand but also in Indonesia; c) disturbances to the division of powers by either authoritarian ambitions of executive leaders (as in Thailand and the Philippines) or the accommodation of illiberal veto actors into the state infrastructure (as in Indonesia); d) attacks on the civil rights of regime opponents and minorities; and e) the re-escalation of communal conflicts, as in Thailand's south or in Mindanao in the Philippines. Importantly, however, in none of the investigated cases was an economic crisis the trigger or even the broader context of democratic peaks ending. Instead, other drivers were at play. But before we can move to analyze the anti-democratic drivers in Southeast Asia, we must first assess the current democratic quality of each polity and describe how it differs from prior highpoints. It is to this task that Section 3 now turns.

3 Democratic Descent

Comparing the democratic peak points of our three Southeast Asian case studies with these countries' current level of democratic quality offers a number of analytical benefits. Most importantly, such a contrasting analysis allows for a clear identification of the extent of the change that has taken place in specific arenas of democratic life – which, in turn, describes the degree of deconsolidation. This approach also provides insights into when exactly this change occurred and what the impact of that change was on the respective polities' regime status. While the main focus is on the trajectory of Southeast Asian democracies just prior to the pandemic, developments during the COVID-19 outbreak are also considered. This integrated approach demonstrates that much of the damage to these polities was done before the outbreak began, but also points to continuities between pre-pandemic deterioration and further anti-democratic trends visible during the pandemic. Significantly, the following analysis prepares the groundwork for the subsequent and in many ways most important sections of this Element: that is, the discussion of the drivers of democratic deconsolidation in pre-pandemic Southeast Asia.

3.1 Indonesia: Illiberal Trends

Recall that Indonesia recorded its historic democratic peak in the period between 2004 and 2008, with democratic deepening occurring in all four of Merkel's consolidation areas. The discussion that follows compares this 2004–8 peak to today's democratic quality in Indonesia, with the difference between the two indicating the degree of democratic deconsolidation that has taken place. As this analysis will show, deconsolidation trends have been visible across the various arenas of democratic quality and consolidation, and this regression has come in the form of increasing illiberalism both at the elite and society levels (Warburton and Power 2020).

In terms of its constitutional order, the current Indonesian polity retains the foundations laid by the post-1998 reform process. But these foundations have been increasingly questioned by elites keen to change them in their favour. For instance, Prabowo Subianto, a radical populist who narrowly lost in the 2014 and 2019 presidential elections, ran on a platform of abolishing all post-1998 constitutional amendments.[5] Similarly, a 2019 initiative for a new round of constitutional reforms included calls by some parties to take away key policymaking powers from the democratically elected president. At the same time, the existing electoral regime has eroded further since some of its flaws marked the end of the democratic peak in 2008. For example, the 'incidence of vote buying in 2014 tripled in comparison to 2009' (Muhtadi 2018a). Likewise, entry requirements for new political parties were tightened further, effectively allowing only actors with considerable resources to join the electoral market (Mietzner 2013). Of the six new parties registering for the 2019 elections, five were led or financed by oligarchs – and even then, none of them made it into parliament. There have also been campaigns, first in 2014 and then again in 2019, to abolish direct local executive elections – the introduction of which in 2005 had convinced Freedom House to upgrade Indonesia to the status of 'free'. Hence, elections continue to decline in their inclusiveness, but even more fundamentally, the notion of their being the only game in town is no longer unchallenged.

The quality of civil rights protections recorded a similar downward trend since 2008, with a growing number of attacks on religious and sexual minorities (Bush 2015). As conservative Muslim and openly Islamist groups gained more influence over society and politics, citizens whose practices do not conform to the Muslim mainstream have been increasingly disadvantaged. Members of Muslim minority communities (such as the Ahmadis and the Shiities), non-Muslim constituencies as well as LGBTI+ citizens have been intimidated by both the state and society. Surveys suggest that Indonesian Muslims' support for the socio-political

---

[5] As will be explained later, this Element adopts components of both Mudde's (2004) and Levitsky and Loxton's (2013) definition of populism.

discrimination of non-Muslims and ethnic Chinese intensified in the second half of the 2010s, especially after the demonstrations against the Christian-Chinese governor of Jakarta, Basuki Tjahaja Purnama (or 'Ahok') in 2016 (Mietzner and Muhtadi 2019). In a sign that this event was part of a broader illiberal agenda, the anti-minority discourse was coupled with a new anti-communist hype. Starting in 2016, the campaign – supported by the military but leading politicians as well – resulted in bans of seminars and intimidation of left-leaning activists (Priyandita 2016). Overall, the quality of civil rights protections is significantly lower than it was at Indonesia's democratic peak in the mid-2000s.

The party system has also weakened since Indonesia's democratic peak. As indicated earlier, oligarchs have become main players in party organization – either by taking over existing parties or by founding new ones. At the same time, institutional shifts in the party system have made it more candidate-centred and less representative. To begin with, the introduction and retention of the open party-list electoral system from 2009 onwards loosened the ties between individual candidates and their nominating parties, making the latter less and less important in elections (Mietzner 2020b). Moreover, the tight party entry requirements (which not only established cost barriers but also favoured ideological centrism) led to a situation in which sizeable constituencies were excluded from the party system. Labour-based parties were among the first to disappear but the increasing exclusivism has also affected the other side of the political spectrum. For instance, many ultra-conservative Muslims no longer feel represented in the party system – especially since their overall influence in many non-party arenas has increased. Surveys showed that about 13 per cent of voters would have supported a new, far-right Islamist party in the 2019 elections had such a party been available (Mietzner and Muhtadi 2018). Thus, Indonesia's party system of the late 2010s not only excluded parties representing poorer and fringe constituencies, it also marginalized orthodox Muslims, who, in response, resorted to extra-parliamentary mobilization. Unsurprisingly, party identification levels fell to around 10 percent by the middle of the 2010s.

The socio-political space for interest groups has narrowed too. In 2013, Freedom House downgraded Indonesia to 'partly free' after a new law on social organizations gave the government the right to ban such groups after securing court approval. In 2017, the government of Joko Widodo (or 'Jokowi') – which had come to power in 2014 by advocating a more moderate version of populism than that offered by Prabowo – even went a step further: it issued an emergency decree that allowed it to ban any social organization without a prior court order. It used this authority to ban the religiously ultra-conservative but non-violent Hizbut Tharir Indonesia (HTI), which had played a key role in the anti-Ahok demonstrations of 2016 and openly opposed the Jokowi government. Not all groups were impacted in the same way and intensity, however. While labour unions retained much of their influence, environmental groups saw an increased level of persecution by the state under the Jokowi presidency (Hamid 2019).

Indonesia's traditional veto powers, the military and conservative Islamic groups, both felt emboldened by and contributed to the rising illiberal trends. As conservative Islam grew in visibility and importance throughout the second half of the 2010s, President Jokowi increasingly turned to the military to counterbalance the former's influence (IPAC 2016). As a consequence, the military gained additional positions and resources, and was able to veto some key policies. For instance, in 2015 Jokowi abandoned his plan to investigate the military-led 1965 anti-communist massacres after strong opposition from the officer corps. As in other countries, the influence of the military establishment grew further during the pandemic, with some retired officers managing the crisis response and soldiers enforcing social distancing (Jaffrey 2020). But as the military's power expanded, the influence of the Islamists did not diminish. On the contrary, they used their ability to mobilize masses as a bargaining chip to pressure power holders. Ultimately, therefore, Jokowi decided to adopt some of their ideas – for example, his police apparatus supported the campaign against LGBTI+ groups (HRW 2018), and he picked a conservative cleric as his running mate in 2019. Thus, even as Jokowi clamped down on the extreme fringes of Islamism by banning HTI, he gave conservative Muslims space by accommodating some of their themes to maintain political stability.

The parallel rise of populism and Islamism was not only an elite phenomenon, but was also reflected in significant illiberal shifts in the norms and values held by the broader population. This increased proliferation of illiberal thought in society cast dark shadows over the existence of a democratic value basis in society, which Merkel views as key to democratic consolidation. As mentioned earlier, surveys in the late 2010s showed that religio-political intolerance among the Muslim majority was increasing (Mietzner and Muhtadi 2019), and similar polls taken at the same time demonstrated that populist ideas were widespread in society (Fossati and Mietzner 2019). Importantly, however, this spread of illiberal values occurred while nominal support for and satisfaction with democracy remained high. Even a drop in the latter measure during the early phase of the pandemic was overturned in the following survey (Indikator 2020: 59). Combined with high electoral turnout as well as strong support for the retention of direct presidential and local elections, such survey data signalled that most Indonesians saw little contradiction in endorsing illiberal values while concurrently defending the formal contours of electoral democracy.

In sum, the broad structures of Indonesia's electoral democracy remain in place and functional, continuing the longest stretch of democratic rule in the country's history. But signs of increasing illiberalism and corresponding democratic deconsolidation are clearly visible, both in elite and societal behaviour – and both prior and during the pandemic. The overall constitutional set-up of the post-autocratic system is increasingly questioned; the party system is weakening; veto powers are regaining previously lost powers; and intolerance and populist convictions are rising in society. These signs have also been captured by democracy indexes. As indicated above, Freedom House downgraded Indonesia from 'free' to 'partly free' in 2013, and in The Economist's 2017 Democracy Index, Indonesia recorded the biggest drop of all countries in that year. V-Dem's Deliberative Democracy index, for its part, saw Indonesia in 2019 at a significantly lower point of democratic quality than at its peak in the mid-2000s, and even lower than in the early transition.

3.2 Philippines: Populist Surge

Previously, we established that the Philippines reached its historical democratic peak in the immediate post-Marcos period between 1987 and 1990, with subsequent phases of relative democratic stability in the second half of the 1990s and the first half of the 2010s. As in other cases discussed in this section, the analysis below assesses the current democratic quality of the Philippine polity and explores the gap between this status quo and the country's democratic peak. Using Merkel's consolidation criteria, the discussion predominantly focuses on the current Duterte presidency, which – according to some democracy theorists – 'perhaps has already crossed the line into autocratic territory' (Croissant 2020).

As is the case in Indonesia, the constitutional structures of the Philippine polity established after the fall of authoritarianism are still operational. But the actions of populist President Duterte (elected in 2016) have severely undermined their democratic substance. The state of the electoral system exemplifies this ambiguity: it remains nominally democratic, but it is eroded by Duterte's increasingly authoritarian moves against elected officials who oppose him (more on this below), and by regular musings about non-democratic alternatives to the status quo. He has routinely threatened to impose martial law (as Marcos did in 1972), and has publicly opined that a dictator would be best suited to rule the Philippines after him (Ranada 2018). None of this suggests, however, that Duterte has openly manipulated elections (such as the 2019 mid-term polls) to cement his power – his approval ratings have been consistently high (at about 80 per cent from the beginning of his term to the time of writing). Similar numbers of Filipinos also supported his handling of the pandemic (SWS 2020), during which he received extra powers and passed a highly controversial anti-terrorism law. Duterte's aggressive populist agitation against democratic conventions and the widespread support it has received indicate a general move away from democratic constitutionalism – while at the same time the formal foundations of that constitutionalism remain standing.

Intrinsically linked to Duterte's questioning of the constitutional status quo, his authoritarian streak has also systematically damaged civil and political rights. Duterte publicly called for the arrest of opponents (including of two oppositional senators, in 2017 and 2018). The police obliged in most cases, which effectively discouraged officials and other citizens from speaking out against the government. Similarly, threats by Duterte supporters against bloggers critical of the president limited the freedom of expression in the online sphere – initially one of the last remaining bastions of anti-government activism (Villamor 2018). Most significantly, however, Duterte sanctioned extra-judicial killings of small-scale drug pushers and other petty criminals. By 2019, official sources put the number of fatalities of this campaign at 5,526, but the Commission of Human Rights said up to 27,000 were killed (Johnson and Giles 2019). As in the case of Thaksin's 2003 extra-judicial killings, the event signified a major step in democratic degradation and deconsolidation (Thompson 2016) – not only if compared to the Philippines' democratic peak in the late 1980s, but also to the Benigno Aquino administration (2010–16). That 88 per cent of Filipinos in 2017 declared support for Duterte's approach to the 'drug problem' is only further testament to the magnitude of the decline in respect for civil rights, both in the elite and society at large (Pulse Asia 2017).

The party system, traditionally weak in the Philippines, eroded further under Duterte. Using the tendency of party representatives to align with the incumbent president to his advantage, Duterte pulled 268 out of 304 members in the 2019 House of Representatives to his side – giving him the largest House majority since Marcos and resulting in the strongest subordination of parties to a president under democratization. Political dynasties also maintained their grip over the local and national party organizations (Vartavarian 2018: 11). In fact, one of their protagonists, former President Arroyo, celebrated a political comeback as Speaker of the House in 2018 – with Duterte's support. Moreover, Duterte continued to build his own political dynasty within a party system serving his interests. In 2019, his three oldest children held important executive and legislative posts: two of them jointly ruled the city of Davao, while another became Deputy Speaker of the House. Therefore, while some replacement of old clans by newer ones took place (Jiao, Calonzo and Dormido 2019), political dynasties have generally defended their supremacy over party institutions. Similarly, interest groups had to accept Duterte's supremacy if they wanted to escape government reprisals. For instance, the International Trade Union Confederation rated the Philippines in 2019 as one of the world's worst ten countries for workers' rights, stating that 'trade unionists in the Philippines faced violent attacks and intimidation ... in an attempt ... to suppress political dissent' (ITUC 2019). Other anti-Duterte interest groups faced comparable repression.

In this climate of increasing illiberalism, the country's two traditional veto powers emerged as major beneficiaries. As indicated above, the land-owning clans (which over time had expanded their influence into other economic sectors too) sustained their dominance in a new constellation, but the security forces actually gained new powers and resources. The police was a main beneficiary of the war on drugs, which gave it wide-ranging repressive authority while protecting the officers involved from legal recriminations. The military, for its part, was given a free hand in the operations against Salafist terrorists following the army's attack on Marawi in Mindanao in October 2017. Similar to Indonesia, the pandemic further added to the armed forces' influence, with the defence secretary heading the coronavirus taskforce, assisted by former military officers (Chandran 2020). Tellingly, Duterte informed the police and military in April 2020 that they had authority to shoot dead anyone who 'creates trouble' during the government's COVID-19 lockdown of Manila and other areas – going much further than his Indonesian counterpart, Jokowi (ABC 2020). Under Duterte, then, the security forces have amassed the most political and strategic weight since 2004, when then President Arroyo relied on military support to counterbalance frequent impeachment threats in parliament.

The strong popular support for Duterte's extra-judicial killings and other authoritarian measures also suggests that democratic values are weakly rooted in society. In a 2019 survey, 51 per cent of respondents agreed that 'it is dangerous to print or broadcast anything critical of the administration, even if it is the truth' (Mangahas 2019). Only 20 per cent disagreed. Many of those who lamented this lack of freedom, however, went on to approve of Duterte's performance as president. They also, concurrently, endorsed the principle of democracy and the way it is practised in the Philippines (SWS 2018). This seemingly contradictory co-existence of democratic and openly anti-democratic values, which Adele Webb (2017) described as 'democratic ambivalence', mirrors a similar complex constellation in Indonesia. But however complex, such an ambivalence still constitutes a significant break from the broad pro-democratic enthusiasm in the Philippines of the late 1980s. To be clear, this break occurred long before Duterte came to power, but his success in packaging populist illiberalism as a form of direct democracy has ensured the further marginalization of substantive democratic ideas.

Duterte's post-2016 populist surge damaged the Philippines' already defective democracy significantly. In all four main arenas of democratic consolidation, it drove a notable decline from the country's democratic peak during the 1987–90 reform era and subsequent, sporadic periods of democratic stability. It is important to recall, however, that Duterte's presidency is not the first phase of democratic erosion since the post-Marcos reform era – the second Arroyo term (2004–10) recorded the country's previous post-Marcos democratic low (see Figure 2). This dynamic is confirmed by the Philippines' democracy index scores; its aggregate score of fifty-nine in Freedom House's 2019 ratings was its lowest since the end of the Arroyo presidency. Given the above analysis based on the Merkel criteria, and in line with Croissant's notion that Duterte may have already entered authoritarian territory, this Element suggests that an even more substantive downgrading of the Philippines would be justifiable. Indeed, V-Dem's Deliberative Democracy index saw the Philippines in 2019 fall to its lowest score level since the collapse of the Marcos regime, pointing to a process of profound deconsolidation.

3.3 Thailand: Return of the Military

As argued earlier, Thailand's historical democratic peak occurred during its only phase of democratic consolidation between 1998 and 2002. It was also already noted how this peak ended in 2003, but the following discussion will demonstrate that democracy further deconsolidated in subsequent years, culminating in full democratic reversals during the coups against Thaksin in 2006 and his sister, Yingluck Shinawatra, in 2014. Comparing Thailand's current democratic quality with its peak in the late 1990s and early 2000s reveals the full extent of this deconsolidation, with the country being the only one of our three Southeast Asian case studies in which consolidation not only regressed, but returned to a pre-consolidation (and even pre-democratic) development stage. Widespread student protests that began in 2020 have challenged this status quo, but thus far the incumbent pro-military regime has contained the demonstrations and held on to power.

Following the end of its democratic peak in 2003, Thailand even lost its first-stage democratic consolidation gains in the area of formal constitutional and electoral reforms – something that Indonesia and the Philippines, in spite of some qualitative erosion, managed to retain. Thailand's democratic order based on the 1997 constitution was thoroughly dismantled through the coups of 2006 and 2014, and it was eventually replaced by a new system designed by the military junta that had taken power in 2014 and governed as a full-blown autocratic regime until 2019. Based on a new constitution endorsed by the junta and passed by a referendum in 2017, Thailand's rearranged political system gave the military and its associates significant veto powers and aimed to keep the Thaksin family permanently away from government. Overall, the constitution created a polity in which 'more concrete power [was given] to an

unelected elite minority – the army, the judiciary and independent organisa-
tions' (Kongkirati and Kanchoochat 2018: 283). In doing so, the 2017 constitution reversed the principle of the 1997 document, which had shifted power
from non-elected officials to democratically elected politicians. Even in formal terms, then, Thailand's post-junta order was hybrid at best and military-
controlled at worst.

At the heart of the 2017 constitution was a heavily manipulated electoral
system that guaranteed that the junta leader, Prayuth Chan-ocha, remained
prime minister after the first post-junta election in March 2019. Under this
system, the prime minister was elected by a joint session between an elected
500-member lower House and a fully appointed 250-member Senate, with the
latter essentially selected by the military. Accordingly, Prayuth already controlled 250 votes in the joint session before Thai voters even went to the polls. In
these polls (which followed a period of five years in which the military
government had banned political party activity), anti-junta parties came close
to winning a majority in the lower House. This was despite regime attempts to
create a legislative election mechanism that would reduce the seat allocation to
pro-Thaksin and other anti-military parties (Hicken and Bangkok Pundit 2016).
In the end, however, even the good result for the opposition did not matter:
Prayuth won 500 out of the 750 votes in the joint session, securing government
for himself and his military associates with the predicted large margin. That he
had to build a coalition with non-military legislators to make governance easier
for his cabinet was a significant nuisance for Prayuth but did not alter the overall
architecture of political control. In delivering continued power to Prayuth
(whose party had gained 23 per cent of the votes at the ballot box), the electoral
system failed to meet even the most minimalist standard of a credible democratic system: namely, that it is the will of the voters that determines the
leadership of government.

Naturally, the repression and limitations visible in the constitutional and
electoral system spilled over into the area of civil rights protections – with
one important exception. Under its direct rule between 2014 and 2019, the
military junta used censorship, intimidation and prosecutions to silence critics,
and it dispersed labour union rallies in addition to banning political gatherings.
While this strict control loosened somewhat after the 2019 elections, it tightened again during the pandemic: according to Paul Chambers (2020), the
military used the pandemic to 'temporarily resurrect its pre-2019 autocracy'
to pursue its critics. The regime increased its repression further when it cracked
down on the 2020 protest movement, especially after October. In this sense, the
decline in the quality of the civil rights regime, compared to Thailand's earlier
democratic peak, has been considerable. It must be noted, however, that the pro-

military government has taken a surprisingly liberal stance on LGBTI+ rights. In May 2018, it launched a Same Sex Life Partnership Registration Bill which, if promulgated into law, would make Thailand the first Southeast Asian country to take steps towards same-sex marriage (The Nation 2018). Given the increasing hostility towards LGBTI+ groups in Indonesia, Thailand's opposite moves should not be discounted, its repression in other areas notwithstanding.

Thailand's party system, which had been historically weak, further destabilized as a result of coups, junta rule and the post-2017 'reform' of the political system. Thaksin's Thai Rak Thai Party, which had been the anchor of the post-1997 party system, was disbanded in 2007, and its successor party was banned in 2008 as well. Thai Rak Thai's incarnation, the Pheu Thai Party, currently operates under permanent threat of disbandment, while another pro-Thaksin party, Thai Raksa Chart, was disbanded prior to the 2019 elections because it had nominated a member of the royal family as its candidate for prime minister. Outside of the pro-Thaksin parties, a new progressive party emerged: Future Forward, led by the young, charismatic billionaire Thanathorn Juangroongruangkit. But, predictably, Thanathorn was disqualified as a legislator over a technicality, and the party itself was banned in February 2020. It was Future Forward's banning that triggered the initial student demonstrations of 2020, before morphing into a larger anti-regime (and anti-monarchy) movement. Prayuth's Palang Pracharat Party, in contrast, is a regimist party unlikely to succeed in institutionalizing itself beyond military and bureaucratic elites. In short, the Thai party system has been damaged by political judicialization (Dressel and Mietzner 2012) – that is, party bans and disqualifications of legislators by the judiciary – as well as the creation of a pro-regime party that has the sole aim of sustaining the grip of the current Prayuth-linked officers on power.

All of the above indicates, of course, that the ability of the Thai polity to constrain its veto powers has dramatically declined since the early 2000s. While the military staged a formidable political comeback, its close ally, the monarchy, also re-consolidated its position. This occurred in spite of the death of long-time monarch Bhumipol Adulyadei in 2016, after seventy years on the throne. During much of his rule, Bhumipol had meddled in politics, including by endorsing coups, but he had initially taken a hands-off approach to Thaksin's democratically elected government (Handley 2006). Subsequently, however, he supported the 2006 and 2014 coups, and his son and successor, Vajiralongkorn, took an even more hardline approach to the defence of royal influence. Demanding (and receiving) direct control over two infantry regiments and more financial autonomy in managing the palace's assets, Vajralongkorn 'vigorously intervened in the political domain … to increase his power' (Chachavalpongpun 2017). While the 2020 protests targeted the monarchy for the first time in decades, it is hard to see a scenario under which the king and his network would be truly sidelined. This toxic combination of an interventionist military and a politically ambitious monarchy presents severe obstacles to restoring functional (let alone consolidating) democracy in Thailand.

Support for democratic values has also declined significantly among the broader population. This has been particularly visible in the Bangkok-centred middle and upper classes, which generally allied with the military and the monarchy in the conflict with Thaksin. As the democratic consolidation climax came to an end in the mid-2000s, an Asia Barometer survey showed that: 'Bangkok residents, in 2006, [were] significantly less supportive of diversity and freedoms generally associated with civil liberties than in the past. They [were] more likely to be sympathetic with constraints on civil liberties, particularly during times of national emergencies' (Albritton and Bureekul 2007: 35). This does not mean that pro-Thaksin forces were inherently more democratic, however. They often held a strong 'contempt' for 'urban, educated, cosmopolitan candidates' in elections, mirroring the in-principle rejection of rural nominees by the Bangkok middle class (Albritton and Bureekul 2007: 30). Similarly, the strong support of Thaksin supporters for the latter's undemocratic policies (such as the extra-judicial killings) pointed to a majoritarian understanding of democracy within this specific group. Although the rise of the Future Forward Party and the student movement of 2020 signalled that a post-junta generation, with a new understanding of democracy, is emerging, the illiberalism associated with previous conflicts remains widespread in Thai society (Diamond 2019: 156). During the 2020 protests, this became evident in the counter-demonstrations by royalist groups that demanded strong action being taken against the protest leaders.

It is clear, then, that the Thai polity has seen the strongest signs of democratic deconsolidation among its Southeast Asian peers – indeed, it witnessed a democratic reversal. It undid its first stage of democratic consolidation by destroying the constitutional and electoral order that had been built on the foundations of the 1997 constitution; it further deinstitutionalized the party system; it allowed its traditional veto powers to retake political power; and it saw a considerable deterioration of democratic values within its society. Even after the end of direct military rule, therefore, V-Dem's Deliberative Democracy index saw Thailand in 2019 at an only slightly elevated level of democratic quality compared to the junta period, and below previous military regimes from the 1950s to the 1990s. However, the emergence of the 2020 protest movement has complicated the analysis of Thailand's democratic trajectory: on the one hand, the protest confirmed the existence of strong post-junta and post-Thaksin democratic pockets among the young generation, which could ultimately lead to reform. On the other hand, it is equally clear that the regime is determined to defend its interests, and it is not implausible that it could survive for a significant period of time by turning even more repressive.

3.4 Southeast Asia's Democratic Decline

The analysis presented in the two preceding sections puts us now into a position to systematically answer one of the key questions that this Element posed at the beginning: that is, whether Southeast Asian democracy was indeed in a process of decline prior to the pandemic, or whether such an assertion was overdrawn. The discussion so far has clearly shown that all three Southeast Asian polities that had seen peak periods of democratic consolidation between the late 1980s and mid-2000s subsequently experienced some form of deconsolidation. The degree of this deconsolidation has varied: Indonesia, for example, recorded a moderate but noticeable regression from its democratic peak in the mid-2000s; the Philippines, for its part, went through a serious process of deconsolidation, especially under Duterte – so much so that V-Dem identified it in 2019 as the country with the highest future risk of autocratization (V-Dem 2019: 28); and Thailand suffered from the largest degree of deconsolidation, regressing from the region's most prospective democracy back to a military-steered electoral autocracy. Importantly, in all three cases, the trends of deconsolidation continued, and even accelerated, during the pandemic. As explained in the introduction, this Element does not specifically analyze the trajectory of democratic quality in Southeast Asia's non-democracies or hybrid regimes, but if all the region's more established democracies are deconsolidating, this must count heavily towards an overall assessment of democratic decline in the region.

The task of identifying the drivers of this process will be carried out in detail in Section 4, but it is useful to summarize some of the common patterns of deconsolidation in the three explored cases. There was a) a persistence and, in many cases, comebacks of old veto players, who in turn benefitted from the survival of pre-democratic structures and institutions; b) the emergence of new populist actors (such as Prabowo, Jokowi, Duterte and Thaksin) who claimed to mobilize against, but often built alliances with, the old veto players; c) challenges to, and active steps to dismantle, the constitutional and electoral order developed during highpoints of democratic consolidation; d) a dramatic erosion of civil rights protections; and e) a proliferation of illiberal values among the population. It is also notable that as in the analysis of factors that ended democratic peaks, there were no extended economic crises (defined here as declines in GDP growth) that caused, or even just accompanied, the periods of deconsolidation.

Having established the occurrence of deconsolidation, and having described some of the phenomena marking it, we can now proceed to a more comprehensive discussion of its causes and actors. In the following three sections of this Element, the analysis of the reasons for the recent qualitative contraction in Southeast Asian democracies will take a more longitudinal and structural perspective than the discussion thus far. Concretely, they will take the triggers of democratic collapses in Southeast Asia in the 1950s, 1960s and 1970s into consideration when identifying the causes of today's decline. For instance, the deep entrenchment of the military in Thai politics since the 1930s, and in Indonesia since the 1940s, will have to be examined in some detail. Similarly, the enduring dominance of land-owning clans in the Philippines, which played a role in democratic decline after the democratic peak in the late 1980s, has its roots in long-standing, even pre-independence social structures. Indeed, as will be shown, it is the mixing of these persistent old structures and players with newly emerging trends and actors that created the specific context for democratic deconsolidation in Southeast Asia.

4 Old Structures and Players

This section begins the discussion of the drivers of democratic deconsolidation in Southeast Asia with an analysis of persistent structures and actors that have undermined democratic deepening in the past and continue to erode democracy today. While there are many pre-democratic societal patterns that survived the democratic transitions in our case studies and played a role in their subsequent deconsolidation processes, this Element focuses on three arenas in particular. Successively, it looks at the persistence of clientelism as a key principle of socio-political organization; the continued politicization of the security forces; and the existence of autocratic enclaves, whether in conflict areas or in territories that are under the control of strongmen (or women). As will be argued later, these structures and actors did not in themselves fail democratic projects, but they provided the foundation upon which newer anti-democratic campaigns could flourish.

4.1. Clientelism and Patronage

Clientelism, understood here as a "contingent exchange" (Hicken 2011: 291) in which patrons offer material benefits to clients in the expectation of receiving socio-political support, has been a key aspect of societal organization of Southeast Asian states for centuries. Colonialism did not disrupt these relationships and practices – indeed, it often made them worse because colonial powers inserted their own clientelistic patterns into the societies they governed (Adams

1996). In modern polities, clientelism predominantly takes the shape of political or electoral clientelism, which "happens when voters, campaign workers, or other actors provide electoral support to politicians in exchange for personal favors or material benefits" (Aspinall and Berenshot 2019: 2). The goods and benefits distributed in such exchanges are referred to as patronage – whether they come in the form of cash, jobs or other material assistance. Clientelism and patronage distribution were trademarks of both the democratic and authoritarian predecessors of the Southeast Asian polities that reached their peaks of democratic consolidation between the late 1980s and mid-2010s. For new democratic leaders, overcoming these clientelistic structures was a key component of their reform agenda, but to a large extent, they failed in that effort. As will be shown below, in some cases, democratic reforms even led to a modernization and intensification of clientelistic structures.

In Indonesia, clientelism had been present during the country's democratic experiment in the 1950s, but it was particularly prominent under Suharto's authoritarian rule. During the regime's stage-managed elections, ministers toured the country to distribute patronage to entice voters to support Suharto's electoral machine, Golkar. But the democratic regime change in 1998 did little to erode the organizing principle of "contingent exchanges" between politicians and voters. Instead, clientelism evolved into a sophisticated machinery, in which politicians distributed both private and public goods (including cash) to voters through a network of brokers (Aspinall and Berenshot 2019). In 1999 and 2004, this trend was still somewhat mitigated by the party-centred electoral systems practiced in those years' parliamentary polls. But the introduction of a fully open party list system in 2009, which encouraged competition between candidates of the same party, led to an escalation of clientelistic practices. As indicated earlier, vote buying intensified significantly between the 2009 and 2014 elections, and it made Indonesia the country with the world's third highest incidence of this form of electoral bribery (Muhtadi 2018). In turn, the increasing cost of gaining political office fuelled a vicious cycle in which political candidates raised money illicitly by misusing their public positions or offered favours to oligarchic patrons (Mietzner 2015). Thus, expanding clientelism was a significant part of the narrative of democratic deconsolidation after 2009, and it made it easier for other anti-democratic campaigns to succeed.

The practice of clientelism in the Philippines is associated with, and reflected in, the continued dominance of land-owning local dynasties. These clan dynasties, which typically gained their landholdings during Spanish and American colonial rule or during the 'emergence of the Philippine Republic as a weak postcolonial state' (McCoy 1994: 434), often hand key political posts in their province, city or municipality from generation to generation. Patronage is the glue that keeps the clans and the voters connected, with the families handing out jobs and other benefits in return for continued electoral support. When Marcos fell, Corzaon Aquino was an unlikely challenger to this socio-political reality, given that she was the representative of a major clan herself. Estrada, a non-clan populist outsider, ruled only briefly from 1998 to 2001, after which Arroyo (who was a member of another big clan) took over, followed by Corazon's son Benigno in 2010. In the 2019 congressional elections, there were 'at least 163 political families whose winning members include senators, House representatives, or governors' (Bueza and Castro 2019). This does not mean, however, that clientelism is limited to the clans. Non-clan politicians engage in the same practice, using *liders* (or brokers) to distribute cash to voters (Aspinall, Davidson, Hicken and Weiss 2016). This ubiquity of clientelism not only prevented democracy from progressing, but also delivered welcome material to Duterte's populist campaign – in spite of his heading his own political dynasty.

Similarly, clientelism, and especially vote buying, had been a prominent feature of the Thai polities preceding the post-1997 democratic order (Dalpino 1991; Callahan and McCargo 1996). Subsequently, Thailand experimented with a wide range of electoral systems to curb the problem of vote buying, with little success. In fact, no other Southeast Asian country changed electoral systems more frequently than Thailand, and yet vote buying has remained 'rampant' – including in the 2019 elections (Bangkok Post 2019). This was caused partly by the fact that the designers of Thailand's successive electoral systems were guided by other, barely concealed interests besides reducing the intensity of clientelism. For instance, the creators of the electoral systems for the 2007, 2011 and 2019 elections were more concerned with keeping the pro-Thaksin parties small than with mitigating the problem of vote buying (to be sure, they did not achieve the former aim either). Obviously, ruling elites – especially the military – had no interest in a system in which voters would elect representatives exclusively based on programmatic ideas. Parties such as Prayuth's Palang Pracharat, which are state-centred in nature and thus almost entirely rely on the promise of delivering government benefits, not only have no interest in reducing clientelism, but they thrive from its continuation and intensification. The persistence of clientelism, therefore, is linked to the preservation of the status quo.

Why, then, have reformers failed to combat clientelism in all three Southeast Asian democracies, even during periods of democratic consolidation? It would be too easy to only point to deep socio-economic structures that proved resistant to short-term institutional change. While such political culture approaches are compelling, it is equally important to highlight missed opportunities for policy interventions. Most essentially, all three polities – when dominated by reformers – were unsuccessful in formulating an effective answer to the key question of political organization: that is, who should fund politics if dependence on government patronage and oligarchic sponsors is to be avoided? For instance, none of the three polities chose to offer significant public funding to parties, making them vulnerable to influence meddling by external actors (Ufen and Mietzner 2015). As democratization increased the cost of campaigning, the pool of candidates became increasingly limited to those who had the necessary resources to run. Once participating in government, these politicians – whether linked to pre-democratic regimes or members of the post-authoritarian class – took further measures to block reform initiatives aimed at reducing clientelism (such as bills on limiting the influence of dynasties in the Philippines). In short, Southeast Asia's clientelistic structures bred politicians who reproduced the flawed system that brought them to power, with reformist forces proving too weak to interrupt the cycle of high-cost elections, clientelism and abuse of public office.

4.2 Assertive Military and Police Forces

Besides persistent and escalating clientelism, politically assertive militaries and other security agencies have also played an important role in fueling democratic deconsolidation in Indonesia, the Philippines and Thailand. (Obviously, the armed forces ended the democratic transition in Myanmar, too.) In Indonesia and the Philippines, the military has regained some of its pre-democratic influence by providing an informal insurance policy to civilian presidents who want to counterbalance their unreliable coalition partners, with the officer corps receiving rewards in return. Some of these rewards have come in the form of additional positions and resources, but also in the shape of presidential support for traditional ideological campaigns favored by the military: among others, for hardline anti-communism and military-controlled law and order indoctrination. In Thailand, the military's resurgence has been more direct: it has retaken its former political leadership role, using the monarchy (rather than civilian leaders) as its main ally. These developments demonstrate that the civil-military relations literature – seen by some as increasingly outdated (Angstrom 2013) – remains crucial to the understanding of democratic decline in Southeast Asia (Croissant 2018).

In the Indonesian case, a long history of military support for anti-democratic orders made it unlikely that the officer corps would easily support post-1998 democratization. In the 1950s, the military had called for an end to liberal democracy, helping Sukarno to establish his autocratic Guided Democracy regime in 1959. Subsequently, it formed the backbone of Suharto's New Order regime. After the fall of authoritarianism in 1998, the armed forces initially accepted democratic reforms because the civilian elite forced it to do so (Mietzner 2009). In Yudhoyono's first term (2004–9), civilian control over the armed forces was strongest. But in his second term (2009–14), as he grew frustrated with his coalition partners, Yudhoyono began to grant the military renewed concessions (Mietzner 2018). Jokowi, coming to power in 2014 as the country's first non-elite president, intensified this trend. He included retired generals from the autocratic era in his government – putting them, among others, in charge of handling the pandemic. The military's re-strengthening amplified the increasing socio-ideological conservatism that spread from the late 2000s onwards, culminating in the state-led criminalization of alleged communists and social activists. The police, for its part, also saw its political role increased under Jokowi, gaining – for the first time in its history – the positions of intelligence chief and interior minister. It also ran an unprecedented and systematic anti-LGBTI+ campaign that reflected hardening societal sentiments against unorthodox social identities. The increased role for the security apparatus, then, returned pre-democratic actors to positions of power and eroded important civil rights protections.

The Philippine security forces have also contributed to democratic deconsolidation without directly taking over government. Less powerful than its Indonesian and Thai (as well as Myanmar) counterparts, the Philippine military was not instrumental in the decline of democracy in the 1960s, but assisted Marcos in stabilizing his autocratic regime in the 1970s and 1980s (Hedman 2001). In a comparable way, but within a formal democratic framework, it helped post-1986 presidents to defend their positions against political threats. This pattern was most visible under Arroyo, when military members were implicated in a spike of extra-judicial killings, and the armed forces mobilized votes for the president in Mindanao in the deeply flawed 2004 elections (Arugay 2011). These actions cost the Philippines its status as an electoral democracy in the mid- to late 2000s (Freedom House 2008), marking an extended period of deconsolidation. The next such period came under Duterte, when the security forces again grew in importance as instruments of presidential power maintenance rather than as independent actors keen to rule on their own. Duterte used the police to pursue his anti-drug campaign, giving it a key role in tightening the government's control over lower class urban areas. The military, by the same token, saw its authority increased in crisis management, including during the pandemic. Duterte, for his part, proudly confirmed that he promoted a 'militarization of government' (Ranada 2018), saying that military officers showed more loyalty in executing orders.

In Thailand, the military has been a protagonist on the political stage since its coup against the absolute monarchy in 1932. It retreated only temporarily in the mid-1970s and between 1992 and the early 2000s, accepting a series of democratic governments that it perceived as non-threatening. But when Thaksin expanded his power after 2001 (McCargo and Pathmanand 2005), the military saw its privileges at risk. In order to challenge Thaksin, the military re-strengthened its alliance with the monarchy. In addition, the generals aligned with the very Bangkok-based middle class that had demanded the army's marginalization in the early 1990s but was now more afraid of Thaksin's redistributive policies (Bello 2018: 45). Ultimately, 'the urban middle class joined the military in a civil-military coup coalition' (Croissant 2013: 273) that first removed Thaksin in 2006, and then overthrew his sister Yingluck in 2014. The armed forces subsequently designed a new polity with institutionalized military privileges and mechanisms to prevent another Thaksin-style figure. In sum, while the Indonesian and the Philippine militaries had no opportunities to take over full power because cross-constituency civilian coalitions would have opposed such a move, the Thai officer corps was able to restore its political hegemony because it found key civilian allies to support this ambition. With the monarchy and large segments of the middle class behind it, the military dismantled many of the democratic achievements enshrined in the 1997 constitution.

As important as the continued power of the security forces was in ending democratic highpoints in Indonesia, the Philippines and Thailand, it is insufficient to exclusively explain the instance of democratic deconsolidation. Evidently, all three countries saw periods of democratic consolidation despite the long-standing influence of their security forces, suggesting that the latter's assertiveness is not a hurdle impossible to overcome. Furthermore, the differentiation in deconsolidation outcomes (from moderate to severe, and from military power sharing to direct military rule) indicates that other factors must have been at play. Like clientelism, meddling by the security forces was a structural deficiency of all three democracies, which required additional developments and interventions to produce the overall outcome of deconsolidation. We will discuss these additional factors in Section 5, but before we do, we need to analyse one more long-term structural shortcoming that contributed to the deconsolidation process: that is, the existence of non-democratic enclaves in all three polities.

4.3 Non-Democratic Enclaves

Authoritarian enclaves in democratic states – that is, geographic areas in which national democratic processes do not apply or apply inconsistently – pose serious challenges to the quality and sustainability of the entire polity (Benton

2012). Not only do they reduce the substance of the national-level democratic system, but they have the potential to infect other areas of the country. In some nations, authoritarian enclaves disappear over time (Mickey 2015), but, in others, they grow and contribute to democratic decline of the entire polity. In Southeast Asia's democracies, the latter has taken place: in all three polities, democratization left a number of authoritarian enclaves untouched, allowing them to fester. In all three cases, non-democratic enclaves became sources of continued instability for the democratizing national-level system, eventually contributing to its deconsolidation.

In Indonesia, as in the Philippines and Thailand, there have been two broad types of an authoritarian enclave: conflict areas and local fiefdoms held by strongmen (or women). In the Indonesian case, the most persistent example of a conflict area trapped in non-democratic enclave status is Papua. There, a separatist movement has challenged the Indonesian government since the 1960s, with democratization only slightly reducing the area's militarization and political repression (Hernawan 2017). Pro-separatist but non-violent activists continue to be charged for treason and sentenced to long prison terms. At the same time, elections in Papua's highlands often consist of tribal leaders voting for their entire community, eroding the credibility of electoral democracy. For many national politicians, the need to keep Papua in the Indonesian fold has justified non-democratic measures, contaminating the national discourse on democracy as a whole. Simultaneously, Indonesia's decentralization process – launched in 2001 – has allowed for the emergence of provinces and districts controlled by quasi-authoritarian politicians and their families. While decentralization made most areas more democratic, in a handful of authoritarian enclaves, power holders established systems with near-total control over the legislature, judiciary, bureaucracy and economy. Occasionally, such power holders get arrested for corruption, but members of their family continue to rule in their stead – as was in the case in Banten (Sutisna 2017). Often local strongmen (and women) cultivate ties to national political institutions to protect their rule, tainting the overall polity.

Similar patterns have remained in place in the Philippines. There, the separatist conflict in Mindanao (also since the 1960s) has long been a breeding ground for militarization, corruption and political manipulation. It was no coincidence that it was in Mindanao where then President Arroyo secured the votes that delivered her controversial re-election in 2004 – which signalled the temporary end of electoral democracy in the Philippines. While the Mindanao peace process (culminating in the creation of the Bangsamoro Autonomous Region in Muslim Mindanao, or BARMM, in 2019) has since brought some stabilization, the area continues to be vulnerable to political violence and engineering. In other parts of the country, leaders of political dynasties have carved out authoritarian enclaves for themselves, ruling their territories like gang bosses (Sidel 1999). While not all of the 163 political families fall into this category, there have been some extreme cases: for instance, the Ampatuan clan, also from Mindanao, was behind the 2009 killing of fifty-eight people who wanted to accompany a political rival of the clan to register in upcoming elections. It took ten years for the masterminds of the massacre to get sentenced in court. Significantly, Duterte used his own long rule as mayor of Davao, where he said he threw someone out of a flying helicopter without being charged (Reuters 2016), as a model for his populist presidency – evidently with great nationwide repercussions.

In Thailand, a significant authoritarian enclave formed in the majority Malay-Muslim provinces in the south, where separatist groups have been active since the 1950s. Not coincidentally, the security situation in the south re-escalated in 2004, after Thaksin dismantled de-centralized governance arrangements that had stabilized the region during the 1980s and 1990s. Many observers believe that Thaksin wanted to increase his control over the south because it had been a stronghold of the Democrat Party – Thaksin's only serious civilian challenger for political power. By re-centralizing governance over the south, then, he apparently hoped to bolster the position of his Thai Rak Thai Party ahead of the 2005 elections (McCargo 2006). But if this was Thaksin's intention, the operation did not go to plan – instead, it produced a major escalation of separatist violence, responsible for the deaths of more than 7,000 people (Deep South Watch 2020). Similar to Papua and Mindanao, the conflict has served as a pretext for the military to defend its resources and political role. In other, non-conflict areas, local power brokers entrenched themselves in quasi-authoritarian zones. According to Sidel (2005: 60), local 'bosses - known as "godfathers" or *chao pho* – have emerged with the entrenchment of electoral democracy since the 1980s' (Sidel 2005: 60). During Thaksin's rise, these bosses felt threatened, and they reacted by deploying violence as an electoral tool in the 2001 and 2005 polls (Kongkirati 2014). Their violent mobilization contributed to the erosion of democracy in that period, and while the military intervention since then has marginalized the bosses somewhat, they 'will not entirely disappear until the patrimonial structure of the state is radically transformed and personalistic fighting over government spoils and rent-distribution are substantially reduced' (Kongkirati 2014: 386).

Non-democratic enclaves have been important factors in the deconsolidation of Southeast Asia's democracies. They prevented democratic traditions from being institutionalized, destabilized reform projects developed by governments and civil society, and offered save havens for anti-democratic forces to hibernate in during periods of intensive democratization. But as with clientelism and politicized security forces, these enclaves were only a small part of the overall deconsolidation process. This process of democratic erosion needed broader social transformations and new actors to develop its full force. It is these larger socio-economic contexts and deconsolidation actors to which Section 5 now turns.

5 Inequalities and Their Politicization

The dominant social transformation that accompanied the recession of democracy around the world, including Southeast Asia, has been increasing inequality. Obviously, socio-economic disparities are not a new phenomenon – indeed, they are a defining pattern of human history and have undermined democratic quality in the past. Even as the third wave of democratization swept the globe, Terry Karl concluded in 2000 that 'gross economic disparities greatly contributed to ... past democratic failures and, despite the current complacency regarding democracy's third wave, they are likely to do so again' (Karl 2000: 150). But the specific character of inequality has changed over time, and so have the approaches of scholars to measure new patterns of imbalances in the growth and distribution of wealth across a society. Initially, many scholars limited their analysis to GDP growth and GDP per capita, believing that both were effective indicators of the prosperity of a society and its citizens (Lipset 1959; Needler 1967). Subsequently, the Gini coefficient of income inequality was used to gain a better understanding about income imbalances in societies, regardless of its overall GDP. But most recently, it has become clear that even this measure is insufficient to capture contemporary inequalities in assets and control of wealth. Thus, analysts have increasingly focused on wealth inequality indicators (as opposed to income inequalities) to highlight the main trend in the global distribution of assets: that is, the exceedingly extreme concentration of wealth in the hands of a few oligarchs. It is this pattern that distinguishes the current form of inequality from some of its predecessors in post-World War II societies (Islam 2018).

In Southeast Asia, this wealth concentration has had profound consequences for the democracies that had established themselves between the late 1980s and early 2000s. This section will show, first, how wealth inequality in the region increased significantly over time; second, how this trend expanded the political power of oligarchs; and, third, how populists politicized these trends of growing inequality and political oligarchization within the context of existing identity cleavages. The end result was a toxic mix of socio-economic frustrations, political narrowing and exploding populist identity politics that ate away at the democratic substance of all three Southeast Asian states undergoing volatile processes of consolidation.

5.1 Rising Wealth Inequality

Measuring inequality is a difficult analytical effort, in both Southeast Asia and beyond. As indicated already, many early political scientists asserted that the key indicators of growing wealth across a society were the expansion of total GDP and the corresponding increase in GDP per capita. Growth in these indicators, it was assumed, pointed to the vast majority of citizens benefiting from economic development and, by implication, to high levels of satisfaction with the existing democratic order. While this belief in the growth–democracy nexus has since waned, the idea that democracies with high GDP growth have better chances of survival remains popular (Barro 1996; Heo and Tan 2001; Córdova and Seligson 2009). This is in spite of newer research undertaken on this subject – such as the study by Kapstein and Converse (2008a) on 123 democratizations between 1960 and 2004. Testing the linkage between GDP growth and democratic outcomes, they concluded that 'high economic growth provides no guarantee against democratic reversal' (Kapstein and Converse 2008b: 62). This finding also echoes in our case studies: Duterte came to power in 2016 when the Philippines' economy was growing at almost 7 per cent a year; Indonesia's democracy started its decline in the early 2010s when GDP was expanding at more than 5 per cent a year; and Thailand, too, was growing at 5 per cent when Thaksin was overthrown in 2006. Thus, GDP growth does not per se produce popular support for democracy – most importantly, because it tells us nothing about how wealth is distributed.

As GDP growth lost its importance as an indicator of a healthy economic basis for a functioning democracy, scholars increasingly focused on income inequality instead (Karl 2000). In this regard, analysing the Gini coefficient of income inequality (where zero expresses perfect equality and one the most extreme inequality) became the standard measurement. Indeed, the Gini coefficient of income inequality delivers a much more comprehensive narrative than GDP growth of how economic disparities can fuel discontent with democratic rule. This is also evident in our Southeast Asian case studies. In Indonesia, for instance, the Gini coefficient grew consistently throughout the post-1998 democratization period and showed a particular spike between 2011 and 2015 (see Figure 4). This was the period prior to and during the 2014 elections, in which Prabowo Subianto used the inequality theme to run his populist campaign for the presidency. In the Philippines, income inequality has traditionally been high, but increased particularly prior to the 1998 elections – won by the populist outsider Estrada with a pro-poor message (Tuaño and Cruz 2019: 312). Subsequently, however, income inequality seemed to decline – including prior to Duterte's election in 2016. In Thailand, the income inequality trend is

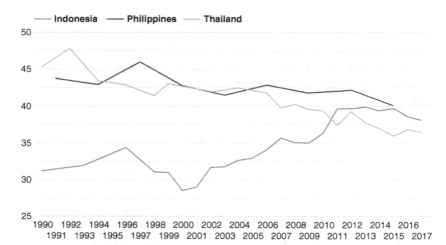

Figure 4 Gini coefficient (income inequality) for Indonesia, the Philippines and
Thailand, 1990–2017

similarly mixed: it showed a temporary increase just prior to the 2001 elections,
in which Thaksin triumphed, but decreased after that. Thus, there is some
evidence that income inequality developed under democratic rule contributed
to successful anti-democratic campaigns, but this pattern is not consistent across
different periods.

   While analysing *income* inequality can't produce the full picture of the anti-
democratic impetus of economic imbalances, the measure of *wealth* inequality
can. Contrary to the conventional Gini coefficient, this indicator focuses on
long-term assets rather than short-term income – revealing compelling (and
worsening) structures of inequality in our three Southeast Asian case studies. As
Jeffrey Winters (2011b) wrote at the onset of Indonesia's democratic decline:
'[W]ealth in Indonesia today is vastly more concentrated in the hands of a few
oligarchs than it has been in over four centuries ... Although [the] richest
43,000 citizens represent less than one hundredth of one per cent of the
population, their total wealth is equal to 25 percent of the country's GDP.'
Oxfam (2017: 1) concurred, stating that 'in the past two decades, the gap
between the richest and the rest in Indonesia has grown faster than in any
other country in South East Asia.' Regarding the Philippines, in 2017 '0.1 percent of the ... adult population [had] fortunes amounting to over $1 million,
[while] 86.6 percent of Filipino adults [had] wealth worth below $10,000'
(Cigaral 2017). In Thailand, a 2012 study found that '0.1 percent of the Thai
population owned 47 percent of the national wealth' (The Nation 2014), while

the Gini index of titled land distribution stood at 0.89 in the same year (Laovakul 2015: 33). Most recently, in 2018, Thailand's wealth inequality index of 0.90 was found to be the fourth-highest in the world (Credit Suisse 2018: 117), recording a twenty-point increase from comparable data collected in 2008 (Davies, Sandström, Shorrocks and Wolff 2009).

As Karl reminded us earlier, the wealth concentration described above did not suddenly occur during periods of democratization. Extreme inequalities had pre-existed during decades of authoritarianism – and in the centuries of colonialism and/or feudalism before that (Robison 1986). In fact, economic imbalances had triggered some of the democratic campaigns against Southeast Asia's autocratic regimes in the 1980s and 1990s. But it is clear that the subsequent peaks of democratic consolidation discussed in this Element did not mitigate such inequalities – rather, in many aspects, they made them worse. The democratic opening not only lifted limitations on civic freedoms, but also on the free accumulation of capital – massively advantaging those who already possessed resources. As we have seen previously, clientelism, the prominence of security forces and non-democratic enclaves persisted during peaks of democratization, making capital accumulation particularly pronounced among the key actors in those arenas (Hadiz and Robison 2004). This, in turn, disappointed many voters who had believed in the egalitarian promise of democracy – an idea that had already been debunked in much of the Western political science scholarship since the 1970s (Jackman 1974) but was still widespread among pro-democracy activists, including in Southeast Asia (Quimpo 2008). Thus, increasing wealth inequalities damaged the popular acceptability of democratic rule and, as we will see below, it laid the path for a growing oligarchization of politics that subsequently fuelled populist counter-campaigns.

5.2 Oligarchization of Politics

The oligarchization of politics – defined here as the increasing political influence of those actors whose primary power resource is direct control over economic assets (Mietzner 2014) – is detrimental to a polity's democratic quality for a number of reasons. To begin with, it limits meaningful participation in politics to those with the necessary capital, shutting out underprivileged actors whose contribution is particularly important in order to reform traditionally elite-centred social, economic and political structures (Crouch 2004; Winters 2011). Further, it allows wealthy actors to dominate policy-making, leading to laws and regulations that protect oligarchs and their associates from prosecution, shift further resources to them and ensure that the system that benefits the affluent is perpetuated. Finally, oligarchization frustrates a number of democracy's implicit claims to the electorate – if not that of fostering equality, then that of ensuring a reasonable level of representativeness.

The steady increase in wealth concentration in Indonesia, the Philippines and Thailand produced such an oligarchization of politics. To be sure, that does not mean that oligarchs fully monopolized politics – but it means that the role of non-oligarchic forces gradually decreased. In all three countries, this process was visible during democratic transition, continued unabatedly during democratic consolidation, and subsequently contributed to, as well as persisted in, deconsolidation. In Indonesia, for instance, the percentage of national legislators who had positions in businesses increased from 45 per cent in 1999 to 54 per cent in 2009 (Mietzner 2013: 95). In later years, this number stabilized, but the economic connections of legislators became increasingly complex – in 2014, each business-linked legislator had, on average, ties to three companies (Iqbal 2019). Unsurprisingly, oligarchization became most intense within the top echelons of political parties. In 2004, none of Indonesia's ten major parties had been led by an oligarch; ten years later, half of them were (Mietzner 2014). Executive elections showed the same trend: the overall number of candidates declined over time, but the role of oligarchs became more important. Prabowo, who ran in the 2014 and 2019 presidential elections as one of only two candidates, was a multimillionaire, backed by his even richer brother – and by oligarchic vice-presidential candidates. Similarly, in local executive elections, only 5 per cent of candidates in 2015 came from outside business, the bureaucracy or elite-level political institutions (Aspinall and Berenshot 2019: 192).

In the Philippines, the fall of Marcos did not halt the process of 'elite reproduction' (Teehankee 1999) within the country's decision-making institutions either. While the 'oligarchy' was far from monolithic and was, indeed, marked by heavy intra-oligarchic infighting, its representatives continued, and increased, their dominance over key bodies such as Congress. In 1992, '145 of the 199 representatives elected were members of political families. The most prominent legislators were business tycoons and industry leaders, and nearly two thirds of the members of the House were landowners' (Teehankee 1999: 2). This trend continued and reached a peak in 2013, when 83 per cent of House members originated from oligarchic clans (Teehankee 2020: 72). At the same time, large-scale oligarchs increasingly entered presidential politics. Manuel Villar, for instance, who ran for the presidency in 2010 and remains president of the Nacionalista Party, has a net worth of $4.8 billion (Forbes 2020). Villar had not risen through the channels of the pre-democratic oligarchy, showing that there were significant changes within the oligarchic class – but also that control over capital (and increasing amounts of it) remained crucial to securing political participation.

This involvement of local-level and large-scale oligarchic politicians not only sidelined more socially rooted actors and thus narrowed the available democratic space, but it also delivered significant profits to the oligarchic class. Under Beningo Aquino's presidency between 2010 and 2016, for instance, the wealth of the ten richest Filipinos tripled to more than $44 billion (IBON 2015).

Thaksin's rise to power in Thailand pointed to similar trends of oligarchic power concentration in that country's post-1992 polity (Rhoden 2015). A telecommunications billionaire, Thaksin took on the traditional hegemons of Thai politics, using his wealth to build a party network and fund effective electoral campaigns (Phongpaichit and Baker 2009). While Thaksin's surge helped Thai democracy to reach a brief peak because it temporarily paralyzed the country's main anti-democratic veto powers, it also predisposed the polity to subsequent decline. Thaksin's wealth instilled a sense in him that he was not only independent from the military and the monarchy, but from parliament, the judiciary and civil society too. Thaksin's career also anticipated a trend, visible in Indonesia and the Philippines as well, that entry into the electoral market was limited to the oligarchy. It was telling that the only serious challenger to Prayuth and the pro-Thaksin parties in the 2019 elections was another billionaire – Thanathorn Juangroongruangkit with his Future Forward Party. While it drew support from pro-democracy, younger voters, Thanathorn's party had been born out of the very oligarchization patterns that had contributed to the decline of democracy. Obviously, the pro-military and pro-monarchy parties were part of this trend too, but they traditionally have access to alternative resources: that is, coercive force and religio-social capital.

While it is clear that increasing wealth inequality and political oligarchization directly wounded Southeast Asia's democracies, these trends have also delivered an indirect, but equally powerful blow to democratic quality. This is because they triggered a counter-reaction by those who used wealth concentration as the lead theme for their political campaigns. Importantly, the most consequential of these counter-reactions did not come – in Southeast Asia and in many other places – from liberal or leftist actors who wanted to maintain democracy while repairing its defects – rather, they were launched by populists with varying levels of autocratic ambitions (Kenny 2019). The role of these populists was crucial as without them, the perception of inequality as such was unlikely to lead to a mass movement for change. Opinion poll experiments in Indonesia have shown that while the percentage of voters who view equality as important increased between 2001 and 2018, the electorate remains divided on whether inequality is rising and on whether the current distribution of wealth is fair or unfair (Muhtadi and Warburton 2020). Most significantly, these experiments demonstrated that the perception of inequality as fair or unfair often depended on a voter's loyalty to a particular political leader or a specific religio-political movement. Consequently, the perception of inequality could be moulded by populists and turned into a political weapon if it became part of a broader attempt to mobilize voters around issues of partisanship and identity. In other words, rising inequality provided the combustible material for an anti-democratic campaign, but it needed populist actors with an identity-centred message to light the fire.

5.3 Populism and Identity Politics

Populists are defined here with Mudde (2004: 543) as those who advance a platform that 'considers society to be ultimately separated into two homoge-neous and antagonistic camps, "the pure people" versus "the corrupt elite," and which argues that politics should be an expression of the volonté générale [general will] of the people'. Organizationally, they 'mobilise mass support via anti-establishment appeals, . . . rise through prominence outside the national party system' and profess to establish a direct 'linkage' to 'the people' (Levitsky and Loxton (2013: 110). For populists, wealth inequality constitutes a key ingredient of a campaign that places the oligarchic class as embodiments of 'the corrupt elite' and themselves as the leaders of the 'pure people' determined to defeat it. But while older versions of populism (such as Peronism in Latin America) had a leftist ideological core, its modern incarnation tends to package the inequality message within the parameters of identity politics. As Fukuyama (2018) explained: '[I]dentity is a . . . moral idea [which] tells people that they have authentic inner selves that are not being recognized . . . . It focuses people's natural demand for recognition . . . and provides language for expressing the resentments that arise when such recognition is not forthcoming.' Populists, then, often appeal to, and try to escalate, these resentments by suggesting to identity groups – which can be based on ethnicity, religion, regional distinction or class – that their position is threatened not only by increasing inequality in general, but by specific rivals from another identity group portrayed as unjustly privileged.

Since 2014, Indonesia has experienced several forms of populism in which this inequality-identity nexus has been prominent. Most importantly, Prabowo ran a dog-whistling campaign in the 2014 elections against ethnic Chinese dominance of the economy (Aspinall 2015). Supported by Islamist groups that shared these sentiments (most ethnic Chinese are non-Muslim), Prabowo's campaign suggested that Indonesia's wealth was looted by foreign powers and their domestic assistants (*antek*), and that many members of the demographic majority (Muslims) lived in poverty as a result. He rarely mentioned these foreign powers and their *antek* by name – but he didn't have to: the anti-Chinese context was clear to most voters. Prabowo's grassroots campaigners even went as far as to falsely claim that his competitor, Jokowi, was himself an ethnic Chinese. While not as blunt as in 2014, Prabowo campaigners revived some of these elements for the 2019 campaign. Prabowo had much reason to believe that the Indonesian electorate provided fertile ground for a populist inequality message framed by identity politics. In a 2018 poll, 54 per cent of respondents stated that ethnic Chinese were too dominant in the Indonesian economy (LSI 2018: 202); in the same survey, 38 per cent of Muslim respondents expressed the belief that they were economically worse off than non-Muslims (LSI 2018: 130). As indicated, perceptions such as these were part of a broader partisan set of values and beliefs held by particular identity groups and thus easily weaponized by populists.

That Prabowo ultimately did not succeed at the national level was mostly due to the 'softer' populist campaign by Jokowi, who instrumentalized the inequality theme by pointing to his own humble background and, therefore, his 'natural' identification with the poor. But Prabowo's strategy nevertheless caused much damage to Indonesia's democratic fabric: the 2016 campaign against the Christian-Chinese governor of Jakarta, Ahok, recycled the narrative of ethnic Chinese dominance over the poorer Muslim masses, and Prabowo's candidate triumphed. The capital's governor, for his part, ended up in prison for blasphemy, showcasing the increased politicization of blasphemy laws against non-Muslims across Indonesia.

In the Philippines, Duterte's populist campaign took a very different form. While Chinese Filipinos hold a position of economic dominance comparable to that of their Indonesian counterparts, Duterte did not choose the path of an anti-Chinese campaign. Picking such an approach would have been less promising than in Indonesia, given that the indigenous–Chinese divide in the Philippines lacks a religious dimension (the majority of ethnic Chinese are Catholic, as are the majority of Filipinos). At the same time, Duterte wanted to cultivate China as an alternative geopolitical partner to the Philippines' long-time ally, the United States. Thus, Duterte instead focused his 2016 campaign on rallying citizens dissatisfied with the power and wealth concentration in 'Imperial Manila' (Ranada 2016). For that, he even emphasized his own minority identity as a Maranao from Muslim Mindanao: 'Screaming "Allahu Akbar!" in his final campaign rally to foreground his Maranao identity' (Curato 2016: 151), Duterte hoped to mobilize every ethnic-religious identity group that felt marginalized by Manila. This was a risky strategy, but was workable in a multicandidate field of presidential candidates in which a simple plurality was enough to win and blocks of minority votes thus carried much weight. But the second flank of Duterte's populist campaign appealed to a broader identity divide in Philippine society: promising a ruthless campaign against drug pushers and general crime, Duterte mobilized fears in the growing middle class of security threats emanating from the poor. Not surprisingly, then, middle-class voters supported Duterte much more strongly than the poor (SWS 2016).

Hence, while Indonesia's populist surge led to a noticeable deterioration in ethno-religious relations, Duterte's campaign in the Philippines sidestepped this arena and instead exploited and deepened divisions between the middle class and the poorest segments of society. The most eloquent manifestation of this aspect of Duterte's populist strategy was the war on drugs, which cost thousands of lives among the urban poor. But Duterte's ambition went beyond that. He also launched a campaign against petty criminals and even just loiterers or *tambay* (Tan 2018). In a June 2018 anti-loitering campaign, 11,000 *tambay* were arrested, with press reports stating that 'most of the arrests have involved men from the metropolis' most impoverished and densely populated districts' (Gotinga 2018). Thus, unlike many of the traditional populist campaigns in Latin America that at least claimed to advance the interests of the poor, many aspects of Duterte's populism have been – in rhetoric and substance – pointedly 'anti-poor' (Punongbayan 2019).

Thaksin's populist campaign in Thailand was more conventional in nature, but it, too, was equipped with an identity element: it appealed to the poor in the north and northeast of the country, and pitted them against the Bangkok-based elites and middle class. Similar to the Philippines, attacking the economic dominance of the ethnic Chinese was not a solid basis for populism in Thailand. This was because they 'integrated into Thai society to such an extent that they increasingly identify themselves as Thai' (Thomson 1993: 408) – and because Thaksin himself was of Chinese descent. Instead, he sensed that there was a huge potential for vote mobilization in the populous but economically disadvantaged areas of the north and northeast – the region in which he had been born and raised. When he rolled out his three-point rural electoral programme in 2001 (debt moratorium, village funds, thirty-bath health care), it did not specifically address north and northeastern voters, but it was clear that it would be most effective there. His main campaign speech in 2001 was littered with references to his being born 'in the countryside', being the 'son of a coffee shop owner' and having attended public school in the north (Pongpaichit and Baker 2009: 85). In his view, this set him apart from the Bangkok elite. Once in power, Thaksin added another identity element to his populism: that is, the disparagement of Malay Muslims in the south after the 2004 explosion of violence there. In one infamous but popular insult, he claimed that some

Muslim detainees who had suffocated on army trucks had died because of their weakness due to fasting (Storey 2010: 46).

Thaksin's populism, therefore, escalated two broad socio-political divides in Thai society that are still visible today: first, the rift between the pro-Thaksin regions in the north and northeast, on the one hand, and the Bangkok elite and middle class on the other; and, second, the tensions between the majority Buddhist Thai population and the Malay-Muslim provinces in the south. Despite the changes that have taken place since the 2006 and 2014 coups, the electoral map of 2019 still showed these divisions clearly. The conflict potential inherent in these cleavages, in turn, remains one of the main reference points for the military when justifying the need for its continued political intervention. Prauyth's much-ridiculed mantra of the need to 'return the happiness, restore peace, and reconciliation' draws, however falsely and self-servingly, from these societal divides (Time 2018).

While the varieties of populism in Indonesia, the Philippines and Thailand played on the wealth inequality theme within different identity frameworks, they all served to aggravate socio-political tensions and undermine democratic quality as a result. To be sure, all populisms described above had been borne out of trends of increasing wealth concentration and political oligarchization that had occurred during periods of democratization, and as such they offered themselves as a corrective to problems democracy had produced. But in most cases, Southeast Asian populists made the existing deficiencies worse. This is because they radicalized rather than mitigated social identity cleavages, and because they often advanced far-reaching autocratization projects hidden behind the rhetoric of representing the 'pure people'. In fact, in at least two of our case studies, the populists campaigning against oligarchic, corrupt elites were oligarchs themselves. Prabowo and Thaksin were prototypes of 'oligarchic populists' (Aspinall 2015) – wealthy insiders who had enriched themselves during the periods of wealth concentration they proclaimed to reject. In Thaksin's case, the self-enrichment continued when in office. Thus, embedded within the continued problems of clientelism, interventionist security forces and non-democratic enclaves – as well as the oligarchization it set out to overcome – Southeast Asian populism has ultimately had a reactionary than transformative political impact. Its contribution to democratic deconsolidation has been significant in all arenas of democratic quality, as systematically demonstrated in Section 3.

The problem of populism in Southeast Asia has been aggravated by the fact that counter-reactions to it have been mostly authoritarian – rather than liberal – in nature. In Thailand, the response came in the form of the 2006 and 2014 coups; in the Philippines, Estrada – who had come to power in 1998 by offering a 'softer' version of populism than its later manifestation under Duterte – was followed by Arroyo's dismantling of electoral democracy; and, in Indonesia, populism was both accommodated and repressed. In Indonesia's post-2014 polity, Jokowi adopted some elements of the Islamist populism that had attached itself to Prabowo's campaign, and after the 2019 elections, he invited Prabowo to join his cabinet as defence minister. At the same time, he repressed the remaining hardline elements of the pro-Islamist and pro-Prabowo constituency that could not be accommodated, banning a major Islamist group and arresting the leader of the 2016 mass mobilization against Ahok, Rizieq Shihab. Even more problematic still, neither the populist surge in Southeast Asia nor the autocratic responses to it would have been possible without the approval by large segments of the electorate. Most prominent among them are middle-class voters, who have played an important role in sustaining the anti-democratic trend in the region. Therefore, the following section will turn to analysing the ways through which this key group in the Southeast Asian electorate contributed to the legitimization of populist and non-democratic rule.

6 Democracy and the Middle Class

In the literature on the third wave of democratization, one influential group of authors explained the increasing number of democratic regime changes from the 1970s to the 1990s by linking it to growing prosperity that ultimately pushed ambitious middle classes to demand more rights and freedoms. In this model, 'democracy is a middle-class consumption good that is demanded once the basic subsistence needs are met' (Appold 2001: 353). Scholars subscribing to this model produced numerous studies that linked democratization to economic growth and expanding middle classes (Colaresi and Thompson 2003). South Korea and Taiwan were often used as case studies (Huntington 1991; Koo 1991), but Indonesia, the Philippines and Thailand also seemed to fit the bill. From the beginning, however, opposing authors expressed skepticism towards ascribing an inherently democratic character to ambitious middle classes. Robison and Goodman (1996: 2–3), for example, raised questions 'about the capacity of Asia's new rich to carry out a genuine democratic revolution and. . . . the depth of its commitment to such reforms . . . The new rich in Asia appear as likely to embrace authoritarian rule, xenophobic nationalism, religious fundamentalism, and dirigisme as to support democracy, internationalism, secularism, and free markets.' Indeed, as the following subsection will show, as much as middle classes played a role in overthrowing autocratic regimes in Indonesia, the Philippines and Thailand in the 1980s and 1990s, they were subsequently also protagonists in those countries' 'middle class revolts against electoral democracy' (Kurlantzick 2013: 28).

6.1 Expanding Middle Classes

While the Southeast Asian middle class was already in a process of growth in the 1980s and 1990s, its development accelerated significantly in the 2010s. This was because the impact of the 1998 Asian financial crisis, which had slowed growth and increased poverty for many years into the 2000s, had been overcome a decade later. Projections made in the mid-2010s saw Southeast Asia's middle class growing from 190 million people in 2012 to 400 million in 2020, as measured by a daily income of US$ 16 to US$ 100 (Leggett 2016: 12). By this calculation, the middle class will have grown from 28 per cent of the population in 2012 to 55 per cent in 2020. In early 2020, the World Bank (2020) stated that in the last fifteen years, Indonesia had 'witnessed its middle class grow from 7 percent to 20 percent of the population, with 52 million Indonesians currently belonging to this group'. Thus, even as the pandemic is certain to slow or even overturn some of this trend, there is no doubt that the Southeast Asian middle class has expanded vastly throughout the 2010s – the very decade in which our three case studies recorded significant episodes of democratic decline that resulted in overall democratic deconsolidation.

These middle classes have two sets of broad ambitions. First, they want to continue their social mobility upwards. But as we saw in the previous section, parallel to the expansion of the middle class, wealth concentration in the top echelons of society has increased as well. With much of the wealth concentrated in a tiny group (as we have seen, only 0.1 per cent of the population hold almost half of the wealth in contemporary Thailand), penetrating this class of the super-wealthy has become exceedingly difficult. Consequently, economic and political oligarchization has presented the middle class with a barrier to further advancement, creating frustrations with the existing order. At the same time, however, middle classes face a second challenge: that is, pressure from below. As the World Bank (2020) explained in the case of Indonesia, there is an 'aspiring middle class – 45 percent of the population, or 115 million people – who are free from poverty but have yet to achieve full economic security. For this group, moving up is just as likely as slipping down'. Thus, a huge group of less affluent citizens are pushing upwards to compete with the existing middle-class segments. These citizens are in a precarious position, increasing their ambition to succeed. Hence, in addition to struggling to advance further, middle classes have to secure their position against citizens who aspire to challenge them for access to socio-economic prosperity.

Such a setting provides an ideal context for populist and otherwise anti-democratic campaigns. As both threats to the middle class emerged during highpoints of democratization, Southeast Asian pro-democracy actors have found it difficult to argue that more democratization will solve these problems. As a result, progressive, leftist or liberal parties such as Future Forward in Thailand, Akbayan in the Philippines or the Indonesian Solidarity Party (PSI) have struggled to mobilize middle-class voters for a democratic challenge to the status quo. Instead, populists or other anti-democratic actors promising to address middle-class problems through radical changes to the democratic system have been more successful. As noted earlier, such populist and anti-democratic campaigns have come in different variations. Duterte promised the middle class to both challenge the elite's grip over 'Imperial Manila' *and* to protect the moderately affluent from threats associated with the urban poor: drug pushing and general crime. Prabowo rallied against the oligarchic elite, and attracted considerable support from the middle class for it. In Thailand, finally, the middle class supported an anti-democratic counter-reaction to Thaksin's specific variant of pro-poor populism, which had challenged the middle class rather than trying to mobilize it. Hence, whether in the form of populism or campaigns to overturn it, large elements of the Southeast Asian middle class have moved to protect their interests by supporting non-democratic candidates and solutions.

6.2 Middle Class Illiberalism

This increasing illiberalism among Southeast Asian middle classes has been reflected in their voting behavior and social attitudes. In Indonesia, for instance, a 2019 survey found that populist attitudes were significantly stronger among high and middle-income earners than among poorer citizens, with populism also increasing with higher educational attainment (Fossati and Mietzner 2019: 782). At the same time, populism was most pronounced among those who had the strongest ideological views on Indonesia's religio-ideological cleavage: that is, those who were either highly Islamist or highly pluralist. These surveys confirmed how anti-democratic populism has been entangled with identity politics – and how more affluent voters helped advancing this populist–primordial amalgam. Additional surveys on religious tolerance found similar trends: in the mid-2010s, intolerance among Muslim voters towards non-Muslim political representation was higher among the middle class than in the poorer strata of society. In a 2016 survey, 50.6 per cent of Muslims with higher earnings objected to a non-Muslim president, as opposed to only 41.5 per cent among low-income respondents (Mietzner and Muhtadi 2018: 484). Recall, too, that Prabowo's radical populist campaigns found consistently more support among the urban middle class than among poor rural voters. Ironically, this was not necessarily what Prabowo had intended:

he had made himself the chair of a peasants' organization in order to appeal to the rural poor, but he captured the more affluent city dwellers instead (Aspinall and Mietzner 2014).

In the Philippines, 2016 exit polls showed that urban middle-class voters had supported Duterte's populist campaign messages much more strongly than the poor – his lead over the second-placed opponent was twenty-six percentage points in the middle to upper strata, and only seven points in the lowest economic bracket (SWS 2016). This was a significant change from the support base of his populist predecessor Estrada, who had drawn 'his support mainly from the lower classes' (Garrido 2017: 650). While Duterte received high approval ratings from the poor too once he was elected, the vast increase in middle-class support for populism between the late 1990s and the mid-2010s highlighted the growing illiberalism in the Philippines' affluent electorate. In an insightful study of this shift, Adele Webb explored the nuances of middle-class 'ambivalence' towards democracy. Interviewing middle class voters in 2015, one year before Duterte's election, she found that the 'dominant reoccurring narrative among respondents was one containing four dimensions, simultaneously coexisting within an imaginary of democracy – that democracy's normative value is freedom, that freedom is earned by embodying a certain restrained behavior, that Filipinos fail to stay within the bounds of freedom, and finally, as a consequence, that it is legitimate for a political authority to impose these boundaries' (Webb 2017: 98). In other words, Filipino middle-class voters reconciled their support for populist strongman rhetoric with their belief in democratic ideals by pointing to the need to impose order on an inherently unruly society.

As indicated earlier, the anti-democratic sentiments within the Bangkok-based middle class grew in response to the threat to its interests posed by the rise of Thaksin. Opinion surveys in 2006 picked up a significant erosion in democratic values in the Bangkok middle class compared to previous years (Albritton and Bureekul 2007: 35). Detailed analyses of these 2006 surveys have revealed a pattern similar to that in the Philippines: as the anti-Thaksin protest grew, middle-class voters viewed themselves as being democratic, but approved of putting limits on the political influence exercised by unorderly poor masses. As Jaeger (2012: 1157) formulated: '[T]hey [still] tended to be supportive of liberal democratic values but they were also more likely to fear the political power of the uneducated majority.' Thus, the middle class broadly endorsed the 2006 and 2014 coups, and it approved of the illiberal 2017 constitution that it viewed as an insurance policy against rule by the 'uneducated majority'. It was only towards the end of the junta's repressive five-year rule that parts of the middle class began to organize against the military–monarchist alliance, with its most liberal fringes supporting Future Forward. This new schism was evident in the 2019 election results for Bangkok: the regimist Palang Pracharat won the most support, but Future Forward and pro-Thaksin parties did well too.

None of this is to say that the attitudes of lower class voters have been much more liberal. Indeed, poorer electorates supported populist surges in Thailand (Thaksin) and the Philippines (Estrada), and while these populist episodes were more democratic than the interventions that ended them, they were nevertheless part of Southeast Asia's democratic deconsolidation narrative. Low-income and low-education voters have also proved susceptible to authoritarian initiatives originally driven by the middle class. As noted, the poorest segments of Filipino society quickly warmed up to Duterte, in spite of their relative hesitance to support him in the 2016 election. Mahar Mangahas, one of the Philippines' leading pollsters, explained that 'while the drug war shows "disregard for human rights", ... what will always come first for [the lower classes] are "bread and butter" issues. And as long as Duterte delivers in that aspect, one can expect satisfaction among the poor to remain high' (Paris 2019). In Indonesia, a similar trend has been visible. While the middle classes took the lead in supporting Prabowo's populist campaign in 2014 and the Islamist mobilization against Ahok in 2016, there was a significant spike in anti-pluralistic attitudes among the poor *after* the 2016 protests (Mietzner and Muhtadi 2019). Thus, while campaigns of religio-political intolerance were largely driven by the middle class, their messaging proved very attractive to lower class segments as well.

These caveats notwithstanding, it is hard to overstate the important role of the middle class in pushing non-democratic agendas in Southeast Asia, particularly since the second half of the 2010s. In what Pepinsky (2017: 121) has termed the 'success of order-first political strategies', middle classes have demanded action against threats to their interests from lower class groups below them as well as from predatory oligarchic elites above them. In many cases, these middle class revolts echoed notions on which previous authoritarian regimes had based their rule: that is, the 'historically rooted belief that political stability and material progress require the elimination of disorderly elements' (Pepinsky 2017: 212). With this, Southeast Asia's democratic deconsolidation confirms the scepticism that Robison and Goodman had expressed in the 1990s about the democratic potential of the middle class. Middle classes, then, are best understood as neither inherently democratic nor non-democratic; rather, they are focused on removing obstacles to their interests, regardless of whether these obstacles are posed by a democratic or non-democratic regime. From the 1980s to the 2000s, middle-class ambitions in our three case studies were largely obstructed by authoritarian power abuse, and so middle-class actors worked towards ending it; from the mid-2010s onwards, however, the character of the challenge had changed. Ineffective democratic institutions proved, in the view of many middle-class actors, incapable of protecting them from new threats, and they hence turned to populists and other anti-democratic actors to step in.

7 Conclusion

This Element has demonstrated that Southeast Asia's democracies have experienced trends of deconsolidation, especially since the mid-2000s. These trends have not been uniform, but involved similar structural phenomena and actors: they all recorded widespread clientelism, politicized security forces and persisting non-democratic enclaves; all of them witnessed rising wealth inequality and an oligarchization of the political leadership; they all saw populist responses cloaked in the language of equality and identity, often by the very actors benefitting from growing wealth gaps; and they invariably have had middle classes disillusioned with democratic track records asking for, and supporting, political alternatives to the status quo. The product of these processes has been the slow erosion (but also low-level endurance) of electoral democracy in Indonesia and the Philippines, and a democratic reversal in Thailand. Populists, claiming to address democracies' shortcomings, have mostly reproduced the order they agitated against, exacerbating old democratic flaws and adding new ones. They certainly did not overcome the oligarchy they proclaimed to fight – they either belonged to the oligarchic class themselves or formed alliances with it in order to build their own crony networks ((Almendral 2019).

The task that remains for us is to integrate this Southeast Asian experience into broader comparative patterns of democratic deconsolidation. One of the motivations for the emergence of the deconsolidation school was the insight that many democracies do not suddenly collapse but fade away in an almost unnoticeable fashion. According to Diamond (2015: 144), for instance, many of today's democratic recessions are not only marked by 'coups, but also through subtle and incremental degradations of democratic rights and procedures'. Although Thailand witnessed two coups in its deconsolidation period, Indonesia and the Philippines declined gradually in democratic quality while their formal constitutional and electoral orders remained intact. Thus, our Southeast Asian case studies appropriately fit into a larger comparative context: they confirm that many contemporary democracies are at risk of slowly decaying rather than being suddenly toppled – but that the era of coups is not yet over either (Croissant, Kuehn, Chambers and Wolf 2010).

Southeast Asia's democratic crisis also followed the timeline of its global equivalent. While the Philippines' descent from its democratic peak began in the early 1990s, Southeast Asia's most recent wave of democratic erosion manifested itself from the mid-2000s. This mirrored the dynamics of the global democratic recession, which is generally believed to have begun in 2006 (not coincidentally, the year of the first anti-Thaksin coup). It was also not accidental that all three Southeast Asian democracies subsequently deconsolidated further in the 2010s, when democratic declines intensified around the world. In this period, the Southeast Asian region recorded Thailand's direct junta rule from 2014 to 2019, the rise of Duterte in the Philippines in 2016 and Indonesia's populist challenges. The two world regions Southeast Asia was most similar to, in terms of their democratic trajectory, were Latin America and Eastern Europe. There, democracy had swept away autocratic regimes in the 1980s and 1990s (as it had in Southeast Asia), but declined significantly in the 2000s and 2010s. For example, Venezuela's autocratization deepened in the mid-2000s, followed by Bolivia's democratic backsliding after 2005 and Jair Bolsonaro's rise in Brazil in 2018. Similar patterns were visible in Eastern Europe, too: democratized in the late 1980s, Hungary saw democratic erosion in the early 2010s, with Poland following about five years later (Greskovits 2015; Krekó and Enyedi 2018). In short, many of the countries that were part of the third wave recorded comparable trends of decline, with Southeast Asia a central part of the deterioration story.

In the same vein, the drivers and actors of democratic deconsolidation in Southeast Asia echo those found at the global level, especially in Latin America and Eastern Europe. Both in Southeast Asia and Latin America, clientelism, politicized security forces and non-democratic enclaves have hampered efforts to institutionalize democracy beyond brief periods of intense reform. In Eastern Europe, long-term structural barriers are different in nature but similarly powerful: there, the legacies left behind by decades of communist rule continue to obstruct full democratization. The patterns of the newest wave of democratic decline are strikingly congruent, too: rising wealth inequality; escalating costs of and consequent limitations to political participation; framing of inequalities within identity discourses; anxious middle classes; and successful populist campaigns – all these ingredients of the decline in Southeast Asia have been present in both Latin America and Eastern Europe as well. Brazil's Bolsonaro and Hungary's Viktor Orbán are representatives of a global prototype of populists who effectively mobilized against democracy's weaknesses, promised to repair them but then aimed to illiberalize the polity once elected. The distinctness of each country's sociopolitical context notwithstanding, then, the Thaksins, Dutertes, Prabowos,

Chavez, Bolsonaros, Fujimoros and Dudas have become near-exchangeable protagonists in the world's democratic recession.

Most importantly, the similarities in democratic decline patterns go beyond those shared between Southeast Asia's young democracies and their counterparts in Latin America and Eastern Europe. Recall that Foa and Mounk offered their concept of democratic deconsolidation as an analytical instrument to investigate what could happen to fully consolidated democracies if they overlooked the warning signs emerging from younger deconsolidating democracies. In many ways, what Foa and Mounk had feared back then is now in the midst of becoming reality. If, for instance, we consider the concept of oligarchic populism as the best encapsulation of what went wrong in Southeast Asia's democracies in the last two decades (escalating inequality, political oligarchization, populist manipulation of identity cleavages), then US President Trump has brought an almost perfect replication of this trend to the United States. Indeed, Trump took the counter-intuitive idea that an oligarch might be best placed to overcome wealth inequalities and oligarchization (already accepted by large segments of the Thai electorate in the early 2000s) to new heights. As a caricature product of inequality and oligarchization patterns, Trump politicized economic disparities in the context of the United States' sensitive racial cleavages, going further than Thaksin and dropping the reservation that Prabowo still had about openly playing the race card. In this sense, democratic deconsolidation in pre-pandemic Southeast Asia was not only a warning of what could lie in store for the West's established democracies; rather, it was an eerily accurate prediction.

Looking ahead, this Element has delivered both good and bad news for the future of democracy in Southeast Asia and beyond. The good news is that some of the region's low-quality electoral democracies have at least survived – as have many of their counterparts around the world. The bad news, by way of contrast, is that the current state of democratic deconsolidation in Southeast Asia – slow and gradual in Indonesia and the Philippines, regime-changing and authoritarian in Thailand – offers few prospects for addressing democracy's considerable shortcomings. This is because the rectification of both the long-term defects (such as clientelism) and the newer distortions (such as rising wealth inequality) would require a significant pro-democratic rupture. Such a rupture, in turn, would have to come in the form of new pro-democracy movements coercing elites to commit to reform. But the likelihood of such movements springing up is, at the moment, low. In Indonesia and Duterte's Philippines, the incumbent regimes successfully sustain just enough democracy so as to not trigger a strong pro-democracy protest movement. In Thailand, pro-democracy demonstrations in 2020 and 2021 have raised hopes of a democratic breakthrough, but the regime seems determined to quell, through violence, demands for radical change. The story of contemporary democracy, then, in Southeast Asia and the world, is one of desperately defending its remaining deposits and hoping to reclaim them where they were lost. The optimistic vision of worldwide consolidation, never stated but inherent in Linz and Stepan's work, now appears like the echo of a long-lost era.

References

ABC (2020). 'Philippines President Rodrigo Duterte warns against violating coronavirus lockdown', 2 April.

Abueva, Jose and Linda Luz Guerrero (2003). "What democracy means to Filipinos", Taipei: Asian Barometer Project Office.

Adams, Julia (1996). "Principals and agents, colonialists and company men: the decay of colonial control in the Dutch East Indies", *American Sociological Review* 61(1):12–28.

Alagappa, Muthiah (ed.) (2001). *Coercion and Governance: The Declining Political Role of the Military in Asia*. Stanford: Stanford University Press.

Albritton, Robert B. and Thawilwadee Bureekul (2007). 'Public opinion and political power: sources of support for the coup in Thailand', *Crossroads* 19(1): 20–49.

Albritton, Robert B. and Thawilwadee Bureekul (2008). 'Developing democracy under a new constitution in Thailand', in *How East Asians View Democracy*, eds. Yun-han Chu, Larry Diamond, Andrew J. Nathan and Doh Chull Shin. New York: Columbia University Press, pp. 114–38.

Alexander, Amy C. and Christian Welzel (2017). 'The myth of deconsolidation: rising liberalism and the populist reaction', *Journal of Democracy*, Web Exchange.

Almendral, Aurora (2019). 'Crony capital: how Duterte embraced the oligarchs', *Nikkei Asian Review*, 4 December.

Angstrom, Jan (2013). 'The changing norms of civil and military and civil-military relations theory', *Small Wars & Insurgencies* 24(2): 224–36.

Appold, Stephen J. (2001). 'The new rich in Asia: mobile phones, McDonald's and middle class revolution (Review)', *Asian Journal of Social Science* 29(2): 350–4.

Arugay, Aries A. (2011). 'The military in Philippine politics: still politicized and increasingly autonomous', in *The Political Resurgence of the Military in Southeast Asia: Conflict and Leadership*, ed. Marcus Mietzner. London: Routledge, pp. 85–106.

Aspinall, Edward (2005). *Opposing Suharto: Compromise, Resistance and Regime Change in Indonesia*. Stanford: Stanford University Press.

Aspinall, Edward (2009). *Islam and Nation: Separatist Rebellion in Aceh, Indonesia*. Stanford: Stanford University Press.

Aspinall, Edward (2015). 'Oligarchic populism: Prabowo Subianto's challenge to Indonesian democracy', *Indonesia* 99: 1–28.

Aspinall, Edward and Ward Berenshot (2019). *Democracy for Sale: Elections, Clientelism and the State in Indonesia*. New York: Cornell University Press.

Aspinall, Edward and Marcus Mietzner (2014). 'Indonesian politics in 2014: democracy's close call', *Bulletin of Indonesian Economic Studies* 50(3): 347–69.

Aspinall, Edward and Made Sukmajati (eds.) (2016). *Electoral Dynamics in Indonesia: Money Politics, Patronage and Clientelism at the Grassroots*. Singapore: NUS Press.

Aspinall, Edward, Michael W. Davidson, Allen Hicken and Meredith L. Weiss (2016). 'Machines and money in the Philippine election', *New Mandala*, 10 May.

Bangkok Post (2019). 'Vote-buying "rampant", says election watchdog," 25 March.

Banpasirichote Wungaeo, Chantana, Boike Rehbein and Surichai Wun'gaeo (eds.) (2016). *Globalization and Democracy in Southeast Asia: Challenges, Responses and Alternative Futures*. Basingstoke: Palgrave.

Barr, Robert R. (2009). 'Populists, outsiders and anti-establishment politics', *Party Politics* 15(1): 29–48.

Barro, Robert J. (1996). 'Democracy and growth', *Journal of Economic Growth* 1(1): 1–27.

Bello, Walden (2018). 'Counterrevolution, the countryside and the middle classes: lessons from five countries', *Journal of Peasant Studies* 45(1): 21–58.

Bennett, W. Lance (2012). 'The personalization of politics: political identity, social media and changing patterns of participation', *Annals of the American Academy of Political and Social Science* 644(1): 20–39.

Benton, Allyson Lucinda (2012). 'Bottom-up challenges to national democracy: Mexico's (legal) subnational authoritarian enclaves', *Comparative Politics* 44(3): 253–71.

Bermeo, Nancy (2016). 'On democratic backsliding', *Journal of Democracy* 27(1): 5–19.

Biezen, Ingrid van (2014). 'The end of party democracy as we know it? A tribute to Peter Mair', *Irish Political Studies* 29(2): 177–93.

Blais, André, Elisabeth Gidengil, Neil Nevitte and Richard Nadeau (2004). 'Where does turnout decline come from?', *European Journal of Political Research* 43(2): 221–36.

Brown, Andrew and Kevin Hewison (2005). '"Economics is the deciding factor": labour politics in Thaksin's Thailand', *Pacific Affairs* 78(3): 353–75.

Bueza, Michael and Glenda Marie Castro (2019). 'MAP: Major political families in PH after the 2019 elections', *Rappler*, 30 August.

Bush, Robin (2015). 'Religious politics and minority rights during the Yudhoyono presidency', in *The Yudhoyono Presidency: Indonesia's Decade of Stability and Stagnation*, eds. Edward Aspinall, Marcus Mietzner and Dirk Tomsa. Singapore: ISEAS–Yusof Ishak Institute, pp. 239–57.

Callahan, William A. and Duncan McCargo (1996). 'Vote-buying in the Thai northeast: the case of the 1995 general election', *Asian Survey* 36(4): 376–92.

Caraway, Teri L. and Michele Ford (2020). *Labor and Politics in Indonesia*. Cambridge: Cambridge University Press.

Case, William (2017). *Populist Threats and Democracy's Fate in Southeast Asia: Thailand, the Philippines and Indonesia*. London: Routledge.

Chambers, Paul (2020). 'Political plague: Thailand's COVID-19 state of emergency as a mere footnote in an historical tragedy of authoritarianism', *CSEAS Corona Chronicles: Voices from the Field*, 12 May.

Chambers, Paul and Aurel Croissant (eds.) (2010). *Democracy under Stress: Civil-Military Relations in South and Southeast Asia*. Bangkok: Institute of Security & International Studies.

Chachavalpongpun, Pavin (2017). 'Lese majeste losing its magic', *East Asia Forum*, 28 June.

Chandran, Nyshka (2020). 'Armies are back in charge in South-east Asia. That's a worry', *Financial Review*, 18 June.

Cigaral, Nicholas (2017). 'Filipinos' wealth declines in 2017 as inequality widens', *The Philippine Star*, 22 November.

Colaresi, Michael and William R. Thompson (2003). 'The economic development-democratization relationship: does the outside world matter?', *Comparative Political Studies* 36(4): 381–403.

Córdova, Abby and Mitchell A. Seligson (2009). 'Economic crisis and democracy in Latin America', *Political Science & Politics* 42(4): 673–8.

Credit Suisse (2018). *Global Wealth Databook 2018*. Zurich: Credit Suisse.

Croissant, Aurel (2013). 'Coups and post-coup politics in South-East Asia and the Pacific: conceptual and comparative perspectives', *Australian Journal of International Affairs* 67(3): 264–80.

Croissant. Aurel (2018). *Civil-Military Relations in Southeast Asia*. Cambridge: Cambridge University Press.

Croissant, Aurel (2020). 'Democracies with preexisting conditions and the coronavirus in the Indo-Pacific', *The Asan Forum*, 6 June.

Croissant, Aurel and Marco Bünte (eds.) (2011). *The Crisis of Democratic Governance in Southeast Asia*. Basingstoke: Palgrave.

Croissant, Aurel and Philip Völkel (2012). 'Party system types and party system institutionalization: comparing new democracies in East and Southeast Asia', *Party Politics* 18(2): 235–65.

Crouch, Colin (2004). *Post-Democracy*. Cambridge: Polity Press.

Curtis, Grant (1998). *Cambodia Reborn? The Transition to Democracy and Development*. Washington: Brookings Institution.

Dalpino, Catharin E. (1991). 'Thailand's search for accountability', *Journal of Democracy* 2(4): 61–71.

Davies, James B., Susanna Sandström, Anthony B. Shorrocks and Edward N. Wolff (2009). 'The level and distribution of global household wealth', *NBER Working Paper* No. 15508.

Deep South Watch (2020). 'Summary of incidents in Southern Thailand, May 2020', *Deep South Watch Database*, 5 June.

Diamond, Larry (2015). 'Facing up to the democratic recession', *Journal of Democracy* 26(1): 141–55.

Diamond, Larry (2019). *Ill Winds: Saving Democracy from Russian Rage, Chinese Ambition and American Complacency*. New York: Penguin Press.

Diamond, Larry (2020a). 'Democracy versus the pandemic: the coronavirus is emboldening autocrats the world over', *Foreign Affairs*, 13 June.

Diamond, Larry (2020b). 'America's COVID-19 disaster is a setback for democracy', *The Atlantic*, 16 April.

Diamond, Larry and Leonardo Morlino (2004). 'The quality of democracy: an overview', *Journal of Democracy* 15(4): 20–31.

Dressel, Bjoern and Marcus Mietzner (2012). 'A tale of two courts: the judicialization of electoral politics in Asia', *Governance* 25(3): 391–414.

Economist Democracy Index (2017). 'Free speech under attack: Democracy Index 2017', Economist Intelligence Unit.

Feith, Herbert (1962). *The Decline of Constitutional Democracy in Indonesia*. Ithaca: Cornell University Press.

Foa, Roberto Stefan and Yascha Mounk (2017a). 'The signs of deconsolidation', *Journal of Democracy* 28(1): 5–15.

Foa, Roberto Stefan and Yascha Mounk (2017b). 'The end of the consolidation paradigm: a response to our critics', *Journal of Democracy*, Web Exchange.

Forbes (2020). 'Manuel Villar,' at: www.forbes.com/profile/manuel-villar /#1c646b7dabb7 (accessed 15 December 2020).

Fossati, Diego and Marcus Mietzner (2019). 'Analyzing Indonesia's populist electorate: demographic, ideological and attitudinal trends', *Asian Survey* 59 (5): 769–94.

Freedom House (1991). *Freedom in the World 1991*. Washington: Freedom House.

Freedom House (2020). *Freedom in the World 2020.* Washington: Freedom House.

Fukuyama, Francis (2018). 'Against identity politics: the new tribalism and the crisis of democracy', *Foreign Affairs*, September/October.

Ganguli, Rajat (ed.) (2012). *Autonomy and Ethnic Conflict in South and South-East Asia.* London: Routledge.

Garrido, Marco (2017). 'Why the poor support populism: the politics of sincerity in Metro Manila', *American Journal of Sociology* 123(3):647–85.

Ghaliya, Ghina. (2020). 'Criticism "not an insult": Police's plan to nab slanderers of govt over COVID-19 questioned', *Jakarta Post*, 6 April.

Gotinga, J.C. (2018). 'Thousands of street loiterers arrested in the Philippines', *Al-Jazeera Online*, 29 June.

Greskovits, Béla (2015). 'The hollowing and backsliding of democracy in East Central Europe', *Global Policy* 6 (1): 28–37.

Hadiz, Vedi R. (2010). *Localising Power in Post-Authoritarian Indonesia: A Southeast Asia Perspective.* Stanford: Stanford University Press.

Handley, Paul M. (2006). *The King Never Smiles: A Biography of Thailand's Bhumibol Adulyadej.* New Haven: Yale University Press.

Hamid, Usman (2019). 'Human rights overlooked as Indonesia's presidential election nears', *The Diplomat*, 30 January.

Harding, Andrew (2001). 'May there be virtue: "New Asian Constitutionalism" in Thailand', *Australian Journal of Asian Law* 3(3): 236–60.

Hedman, Eva-Lotta E. (2001). 'The Philippines: not so military, not so civil', in *Coercion and Governance: the Declining Political Role of the Military in Asia*, ed. Muthiah Alagappa. Stanford: Stanford University Press, pp. 165–86.

Hedman, Eva-Lotta E. (2006). *In the Name of Civil Society: From Free Election Movements to People Power in the Philippines.* Honolulu: University of Hawaii Press.

Heo, Uk and Alexander C. Tan (2001). 'Democracy and economic growth: a causal analysis', *Comparative Politics* 33(4): 463–73.

Hernandez, Carolina G. (1988). 'The Philippines in 1987: challenges of redemocratization', *Asian Survey* 28(2): 229–41.

Hernawan, Budi (2017). *Torture and Peacebuilding in Indonesia: The Case of Papua.* London: Routledge.

Hicken, Allen (2011). 'Clientelism', *Annual Review of Political Science* 14(1): 289–310.

Hicken, Allen (2014). 'Party and party system institutionalization in the Philippines', in *Party System Institutionalization in Asia: Democracies, Autocracies and the Shadows of the Past*, eds. Allen Hicken and Erik Kuhonta. Cambridge: Cambridge University Press, pp. 307–27.

Hicken, Allen and Bangkok Pundit (2016). 'The effects of Thailand's proposed electoral system', *Asian Correspondent*, 10 February.

Holmes, Ronald D. and Paul D. Hutchcroft (2020). 'A failure of execution', *Inside Story*, 4 April.

Horowitz, Donald L. (2013). *Constitutional Change and Democracy in Indonesia*. Cambridge: Cambridge University Press.

HRW (Human Rights Watch) (2018). '"Scared in public and now no privacy": human rights and public health impacts of Indonesia's anti-LGBT moral panic', Human Rights Watch.

HRW (Human Rights Watch) (2020). 'Thailand: COVID-19 clampdown on free speech', Human Rights Watch.

Huntington, Samuel P. (1991). 'Democracy's third wave', *Journal of Democracy* 2(2): 12–34.

Hutchcroft, Paul. D (2008). 'The Arroyo imbroglio in the Philippines', *Journal of Democracy* 19(1): 141–55.

IBON (2015). 'Aquino legacy: wealth of richest tripled', 24 July.

Indikator (2020). 'Perubahan opini publik terhadap COVID-19: dari dimensi kesehatan ke ekonomi? Temuan survei nasional: 13–16 Juli 2020', Indikator.

IPAC (Institute for Policy Analysis of Conflict) (2016). 'Update on the Indonesian military's influence', *IPAC Report* No.26.

Iqbal, Muhammad (2019). 'Makin banyak pengusaha rangkap jadi politisi, berbahayakah?', *CBNC Indonesia*, 7 October.

Islam, Mhd. Rabiul (2018). 'Wealth inequality, democracy and economic freedom', *Journal of Comparative Economics* 46(4): 920–35.

ITUC (International Trade Union Confederation) (2019). 'The 2019 ITUC Global Rights Index: the world's worst countries for workers', ITUC.

Jackman, Robert W. (1974). 'Political democracy and social equality: a comparative analysis', *American Sociological Review*, 39(1): 29–45.

Jaeger, Kai (2012). 'Why did Thailand's middle class turn against a democratically elected government? The information-gap hypothesis', *Democratization* 19(6): 1138–65.

Jaffrey, Sana (2020). 'Coronavirus blunders in Indonesia turn crisis into catastrophe', *Carnegie Commentary*, 29 April.

Johnson, Howard and Christopher Giles (2019). 'Philippines drug war: do we know how many have died?', *BBC*, 12 November.

Kapstein, Ethan B. and Nathan Converse (2008a). 'Young democracies in the balance: lessons for the international community', Center for Global Development Brief.

Kapstein, Ethan B. and Nathan Converse (2008b). 'Why democracies fail', *Journal of Democracy* 19(4): 57–68.

Karl, Terry Lynn (2000). 'Economic inequality and democratic instability', *Journal of Democracy* 11(1): 149–56.

Kenny, Paul (2019). *Populism in Southeast Asia.* Cambridge: Cambridge University Press.

Kimura, Masataka (1991). 'Martial law and the realignment of political parties in the Philippines (September 1972–February 1986): with a case in the province of Batangas', *Southeast Asian Studies* 29(2): 205–26.

King, Dwight Y. (2003). *Half-Hearted Reform: Electoral Institutions and the Struggle for Democracy in Indonesia.* Westport: Praeger.

Klein, James R. (1998). 'The constitution of the Kingdom of Thailand, 1997: a blueprint for participatory democracy', The Asia Foundation.

Kofi Annan Foundation (2017). *Democracy in Southeast Asia: Achievements, Challenges and Prospects.* Geneva: Kofi Annan Foundation.

Kongkirati, Prajak (2014). 'The rise and fall of electoral violence in Thailand: changing rules, structures and power landscapes, 1997–2011', *Contemporary Southeast Asia* 36(3): 386–416.

Kongkirati, Prajak and Veerayooth Kanchoocha (2018). 'The Prayuth regime: embedded military and hierarchical capitalism in Thailand' *TRaNS: Trans-Regional and National Studies of Southeast Asia* 6(2): 279–305.

Koo, Hagen (1991). 'Middle classes, democratization and class formation: the case of South Korea', *Theory and Society* 20(4): 485–509.

Kostelka, Filip (2017). 'Does democratic consolidation lead to a decline in voter turnout? Global evidence since 1939', *American Political Science Review* 111(4): 653–67.

Krekó, Péter and Zsolt Enyedi (2018). 'Orbán's laboratory of illiberalism', *Journal of Democracy* 29(3): 39–51.

Kuhonta, Erik Martinez (2008). 'The paradox of Thailand's 1997 "people's constitution": be careful what you wish for', *Asian Survey* 48(3): 373–92.

Kurlantzick, Joshua (2003). 'Democracy endangered: Thailand's Thaksin flirts with dictatorship', *Current History* 102(665): 285–90.

Kurlantzick, Joshua (2013). *Democracy in Retreat: The Revolt of the Middle Class and the Worldwide Decline of Representative Government.* New Haven: Yale University Press.

Lancaster, Caroline (2014).'"The iron law of Erdogan: the decay from intra-party democracy to personalistic rule', *Third World Quarterly* 35(9): 1672–90.

Laovakul, Duangmanee (2015). 'Concentration of land and other wealth in Thailand', in *Unequal Thailand: Aspects of Income, Wealth and Power*, eds. Pasuk Phongpaichit and Chris Baker. Singapore: NUS Press, pp. 32–42.

Leggett, Regan (2016). 'Asia 2020: progressing, prepared or pessimistic?', Nielsen Future Business Sentiment Survey.

Levitsky, Steven and James Loxton. (2013). 'Populism and competitive authoritarianism in the Andes', *Democratization* 20(1): 107–36.

Lipset, Seymour M. (1959). 'Some social requisites of democracy', *American Political Science Review* 53: 69–105.

Lührmann, Anna and Staffan I. Lindberg. (2019). 'A third wave of autocratization is here: what is new about it?', *Democratization* 26 (7): 1095–113.

Maeda, Ko (2016). 'Honeymoon or consolidation, or both?: time dependence of democratic durability', *Democratization* 23(4): 575–91.

Mangahas, Mahar (2019). 'Surveys of freedom to dissent', *Philippine Inquirer*, 3 August.

McCargo, Duncan (2006). 'Thaksin and the resurgence of violence in the Thai South: network monarchy strikes back?', *Critical Asian Studies* 38(1): 39–71.

McCargo, Duncan and Ukrist Pathmanand (2005). *The Thaksinization of Thailand*. Copenhagen: NIAS Press.

McCoy, Alfred W. (1994). *An Anarchy of Families: State and Family in the Philippines*. Manila: Ateneo de Manila University Press.

McCoy, Jennifer and William C. Smith (1995). 'From deconsolidation to reequilibration? Prospects for democratic renewal in Venezuela', in *Venezuela: Democracy Under Stress*, eds. Jennifer McCoy, Andrés Serbin, William C. Smith and Andrés Stambouli. Miami: University of Miami, pp. 237–83.

Merkel, Wolfgang (2014). 'Is there a crisis of democracy?', *Democratic Theory* 1(2): 11–15.

Merkel, Wolfgang (2018a). 'Challenge or crisis of democracy', in *Democracy and Crisis: Challenges in Turbulent Times*, eds. Wolfgang Merkel and Sascha Kneip. Heidelberg: Springer, 1pp. –28.

Merkel, Wolfgang (2018b). 'Conclusion: is the crisis of democracy an invention?', in *Democracy and Crisis: Challenges in Turbulent Times*, eds. Wolfgang Merkel and Sascha Kneip. Heidelberg: Springer, pp. 349–67.

Mickey, Robert (2015). *Paths Out of Dixie: The Democratization of Authoritarian Enclaves in America's Deep South, 1944–1972*. Princeton: Princeton University Press.

Mietzner, Marcus (2009). *Military Politics, Islam and the State in Indonesia: From Turbulent Transition to Democratic Consolidation*. Leiden: KITLV Press.

Mietzner, Marcus (2013). *Money, Power and Ideology: Political Parties in Post-Authoritarian Indonesia*. Honolulu: Hawaii University Press.

Mietzner, Marcus (2014). 'Oligarchs, politicians and activists: contesting party politics in post-Suharto Indonesia', in *Beyond Oligarchy: Wealth, Power and Contemporary Indonesian Politics*, eds. Michele Ford and Thomas B. Pepinsky. Ithaca: Cornell Southeast Asia Program Publications, pp. 99–116.

Mietzner, Marcus (2015). 'Dysfunction by design: political finance and corruption in Indonesia', *Critical Asian Studies* 47(4): 587–610.

Mietzner, Marcus (2018). 'The Indonesian armed forces, coalitional presidentialism and democratization', in *Routledge Handbook of Contemporary Indonesia*, ed. Robert W. Hefner. London: Routledge, pp. 140–50.

Mietzner, Marcus (2020a). 'Populist anti-scientism, religious polarisation and institutionalised corruption: how Indonesia's democratic decline shaped its COVID-19 response', *Journal of Current Southeast Asian Affairs* 39(2): 227–49.

Mietzner, Marcus (2020b). 'Authoritarian innovations in Indonesia: electoral narrowing, identity politics and executive illiberalism', *Democratization* 27 (6): 1021–36.

Mietzner, Marcus and Burhanuddin Muhtadi (2018). 'Explaining the 2016 Islamist mobilisation in Indonesia: religious intolerance, militant groups and the politics of accommodation', *Asian Studies Review* 42(3): 479–97.

Mietzner, Marcus and Burhanuddin Muhtadi (2019). 'The mobilization of intolerance and its trajectories: Indonesian Muslims' views of religious minorities and ethnic Chinese', in *Contentious Belonging: The Place of Minorities in Indonesia*, eds. Greg Fealy and Ronit Ricci. Singapore: ISEAS-Yusuf Ishak Institute, pp. 155–74.

Mudde, Cas (2004). 'The populist zeitgeist', *Government and Opposition* 39 (4): 541–63.

Muhtadi, Burhanuddin (2018). 'Indonesia's open-list voting system opens the door to vote buying', *East Asia Forum*, 7 August.

Muhtadi, Burhanuddin (2019). *Vote Buying in Indonesia: The Mechanics of Electoral Bribery*. Basingstoke: Palgrave.

Nation, The (2014). 'Richest 0.1% own half of nation's assets', 23 September.

Nation, The (2018). 'Gay relationships bill should be passed by November, experts believe', 9 July.

Norris, Pippa (2017). 'Is Western democracy backsliding? Diagnosing the risks', *Journal of Democracy*, Web Exchange.

O'Donnell, Guillermo (1996). 'Illusions about consolidations', *Journal of Democracy* 7(2): 34–51.

Overholt, William H. (2017). 'Duterte, democracy and defense', *Brookings Southeast Asia View Report*.

Oxfam (2017). 'Towards a more equal Indonesia', *Oxfam Briefing Paper*, February.

Paris, Janella (2019). 'Duterte and the poor: what the surveys say', *Rappler*, 30 June.

Pepinsky, Thomas (2017). 'Southeast Asia: voting against disorder', *Journal of Democracy* 28(2): 120–31.

Pepinsky, Thomas (2020). 'Decoupling governance and democracy: the challenge of authoritarian development in Southeast Asia'" *Brookings Institution Report*, July.

Pew Research Center (2013). *The World's Muslims: Religion, Politics and Society*. Washington: Pew Research Center.

Phongpaichit, Pasuk and Chris Baker (2009). *Thaksin*. Bangkok: Silkworm Books.

Power, Tom (2018). 'Jokowi's authoritarian turn', *New Mandala*, 9 October.

Priyandita, Gatra (2016). 'Behind Indonesia's red scare', *The Diplomat*, 14 June.

Pulse Asia (2017). 'Nationwide survey on the campaign against illegal drugs', Press release, September 2017.

Punongbayan, J.C. (2019). 'How Duterte's drug war is negating key anti-poverty programs', *Rappler*, 17 October.

Quimpo, Nathan Gilbert (2008). *Contested Democracy and the Left in the Philippines after Marcos*. New Haven: Yale University Southeast Asian Studies.

Ranada, Pia (2016). 'Duterte: Roxas perpetuates Manila-centrism', *Rappler*, 30 March.

Ranada, Pia (2018). 'Duterte says PH "better off with dictator" than Robredo', *Rappler*, 30 August.

Reuters (2016). 'Philippine leader says once threw man from helicopter, would do it again', 29 September.

Rhoden, T.F. (2015). 'Oligarchy in Thailand?', *Journal of Current Southeast Asian Affairs* 34(1): 3–25.

Robison, Richard and David S.G. Goodman (1996). *The New Rich in Asia: Mobile Phones, McDonalds and Middle-class Revolution*. London: Routledge.

Robison, Richard and Vedi R. Hadiz (2004). *Reorganising Power in Indonesia: The Politics of Oligarchy in an Age of Markets*. London: Routledge.

Rodan, Garry. (2018). *Participation without Democracy: Containing Conflict in Southeast Asia*. New York: Cornell University Press.

Schmidt, Vivien A. (2015). *The Eurozone's Crisis of Democratic Legitimacy: Can the EU Rebuild Public Trust and Support for European Economic Integration?* Brussels: European Commission.

Sidel, John T. (1999). *Capital, Coercion and Crime: Bossism in the Philippines*, Stanford: Stanford University Press.

Sidel, John T. (2005). 'Bossism and democracy in the Philippines, Thailand and Indonesia: towards an alternative framework for the study of "local strongmen"', in *Politicising Democracy: The New Local Politics of Democratisation*, eds. John Harriss, Kristian Stokke and Olle Törnquist. Basingstoke: Palgrave, pp. 51–74.

Slater, Dan (2008). 'Can Leviathan be democratic? Competitive elections, robust mass politics and state infrastructural power', *Studies in Comparative International Development* 43 (3–4): 252–72.

Slater, Dan (2017). 'Dictatorship versus democracy in Southeast Asia'" *The News Lens*, 29 October.

Solt, Frederick (2008). 'Economic inequality and democratic political engagement', *American Journal of Political Science* 52(1): 48–60.

Spanje, Joost van (2010). 'Contagious parties: anti-immigration parties and their impact on other parties' immigration stances in contemporary Western Europe', *Party Politics* 16(5): 563–86.

Storey, Ian (2008). 'Southern discomfort: separatist conflict in the Kingdom of Thailand', *Asian Affairs* 35(1): 31–52.

Stromseth, Jonathan and Hunter Marston (2019). 'Democracy at a crossroads in Southeast Asia: great power rivalry meets domestic governance', *Brookings Policy Brief*, February.

Sutisna, Agus (2018). 'The proliferation symptoms of political dynasties in Banten under the era of Governor Ratu Atut Chosiyah', *Diponegoro Law Review* 3(2): 182–98.

SWS (Social Weather Station) (2016). 'Exit poll, votes for president', unpublished.

SWS (Social Weather Station) (2018). 'Third quarter 2018 Social Weather survey', 4 October.

SWS (Social Weather Station) (2020). 'Covid-19 mobile phone survey: 84% say strict stay-at-home measures due to Covid-19 are worth it', *Report* No. 7, 4–10 May.

Tan, Rebecca (2018). 'President Duterte waged a war against drug suspects. Next up? Street loiterers', *Washington Post*, 3 July.

Teehankee, Julio (1999). 'Power bequeathed: generational shift and elite reproduction in the 11th House of Representatives', *Occasional Paper* No. 16, Institute for Popular Democracy,

Teehankee, Julio (2020). 'The 2019 midterm elections in the Philippines: party system pathologies and Duterte's populist mobilization', *Asian Journal of Comparative Politics* 5(1): 69–81.

Thabchumpon, Naruemon and Duncan McCargo (2011). 'Urbanized villagers in the 2010 Thai redshirt protests: not just poor farmers?', *Asian Survey* 51(6): 993–1018.

Thompson, Mark R. (1996). 'Off the endangered list: Philippine democratization in comparative perspective', *Comparative Politics* 28(2): 179–205.

Thompson, Mark R. (2016). 'Bloodied democracy: Duterte and the death of liberal reformism in the Philippines', *Journal of Current Southeast Asian Affairs* 35(3): 39–68.

Thomson, Curtis N. (1993). 'Political identity among Chinese in Thailand', *Geographical Review* 83(4): 397–409.

Time (2018). 'Thailand PM Prayuth Chan-ocha on turning to China over the U.S.', 21 June.

Tomsa, Dirk (2010). 'The Indonesian party system after the 2009 elections: towards stability?', in *Problems of Democratisation in Indonesia: Elections, Institutions and Society*, eds.Edward Aspinall and Marcus Mietzner. Singapore: ISEAS, pp. 141–59.

Tsebelis, George (2002). *Veto Players: How Political Institutions Work*. Princeton: Princeton University Press.

Tuaño, Philip Arnold and Jerik Cruz (2019). 'Structural inequality in the Philippines: oligarchy, (im)mobility and economic transformation', *Journal of Southeast Asian Economies* 36(3): 304–28.

Ufen, Andreas and Marcus Mietzner (2015). 'Political finance regimes in Southeast Asia: introduction', *Critical Asian Studies* 47(4): 558–63.

Vartavarian, Mesrob (2018). 'Rodrigo Duterte and the Philippine presidency: rupture or cyclicity?', *IIAS Newsletter* No. 80.

Villamor, Filipe (2018). 'To criticize Duterte in public, "inhale courage and exhale fear"' *New York Times*, 19 January.

Warburton, Eve and Thomas Power (eds.) (2020). *Democracy in Indonesia: From Stagnation to Regression?* Singapore: ISEAS – Yusuf Ishak Institute.

Watts, John. (2018). 'Cause to celebrate democracy in Southeast Asia', *Atlantic Council*, 17 May.

Weiss, Meredith (2020). *The Roots of Resilience: Party Machines and Grassroots Politics in Southeast Asia*. New York: Cornell University Press.

Webb, Adele (2017). 'Why are the middle class misbehaving?: exploring democratic ambivalence and authoritarian nostalgia', *Philippine Sociological Review* 65: 77–102.

Winters, Jeffrey A. (2011a). *Oligarchy*. Cambridge: Cambridge University Press.

Winters, Jeffrey A. (2011b). 'Who will tame the oligarchs?', *Inside Indonesia* 104, April–June.

World Bank (2020). 'Expanding middle class key for Indonesia's future', World Bank, 30 January.

V-Dem (2015). 'Measuring high level democratic principles using the V-Dem data', V-Dem, May.

Yoshifumi, Tamada (2014). 'When election results count: a reflection on de-democratization in Thailand', *Asian and African Area Studies* 14 (1): 96–110.

Cambridge Elements ≡

Elements in Politics and Society in Southeast Asia

Edward Aspinall
Australian National University
Edward Aspinall is a professor of politics at the Coral Bell School of Asia-Pacific Affairs,
Australian National University. A specialist of Southeast Asia, especially Indonesia, much of
his research has focused on democratisation, ethnic politics and civil society in Indonesia
and, most recently, clientelism across Southeast Asia.

Meredith L. Weiss
University at Albany, SUNY
Meredith L. Weiss is Professor of Political Science at the University at Albany, SUNY. Her
research addresses political mobilization and contention, the politics of identity and
development, and electoral politics in Southeast Asia, with particular focus on Malaysia and
Singapore.

About the series
Elements in Politics and Society in Southeast Asia includes both country-specific and
thematic studies on one of the world's most dynamic regions. Each title, written by
a leading scholar of that country or theme, combines a succinct, comprehensive,
up-to-date overview of debates in the scholarly literature with original analysis and
a clear argument.

Cambridge Elements ≡

Elements in Politics and Society in Southeast Asia

A full series listing is available at: www.cambridge.org/emup